MICHAEL JACKSON
KING OF POP

By Chris Cardell

**Project co-ordinator, research
and U.S.A. photography, Gail Johnson.**

JAM BOOKS LONDON

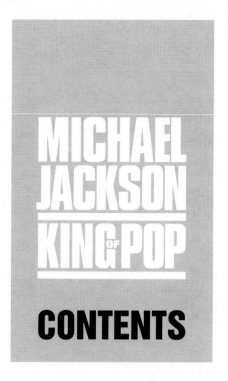

CONTENTS

© Chris Cardell 1992
Published by JAM BOOKS, LONDON.
72 New Bond Street, London W1Y 9DD.

ISBN 0 9519319 0 3
Edited by Linda Cardell.
Designed by Roger Altass and George Damerum of Creative Services Unit, London.
Printed by Brettenham Print, London.
Photographs supplied by: The Press Association, Associated Press, All Action, Alpha, Famous, London Features, Relay, Retna, Scope, Syndication International.

This book is dedicated to my family, Gail's mum,
Stevie and Shane's bank account and Brian Sheppard for teaching me to read and write.
Chris Cardell 1992

The publishers would like to thank Roger Baker and Steve Ronchetti at CSU,
whose help and support enabled this book to be published.

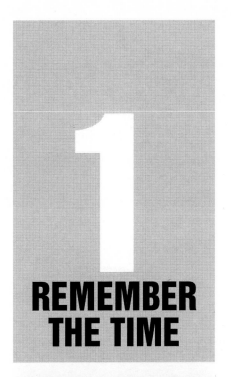

1
REMEMBER THE TIME

Four year old Michael Jackson sat in the corner of the family's small living room looking with envy at his older brothers: Jackie aged eleven, Tito, nine and Jermaine, eight. Just like every other day after school, the three older boys were rehearsing their band, working through their favourite soul classics, with Tito strumming away on guitar and Jackie and Jermaine singing and dancing. They practised hard and sounded as slick and professional as many performers three times their age. Their father Joe was working late at the steelmill. Their mother Katherine looked on proudly as the boys sang their hearts out. Michael was allowed to watch, just as long as he did not interfere. But this time the music was having an effect on him that he could not control. It was as if it were urging his legs to dance, forcing his voice to burst into song. As his older brothers launched into a cover version of one of their James Brown numbers, Michael could contain himself no longer. He leapt onto his feet and started to dance. To his amazed audience it seemed that a mystery force had taken hold of Michael's body. He twisted and turned, jumped and jived, his feet gliding across the

living room floor with the ease of a superstar.

Then Michael began to sing. His golden voice filled the room, he hit the notes perfectly and the words just rolled off his tongue. Tito, Jackie and Jermaine stared in astonishment at their younger brother. His mother just shook her head in disbelief. The little four year old looked up with a smile as he realised that his performance had gone down well.

This was a very special moment and Michael Jackson knew it.

Michael Joseph Jackson was born on 29 August 1958 in Gary, Indiana, a large, run down city

about an hour and a half's drive from Chicago.

In the 1950s, life in Gary revolved around the steelworks. It provided employment for thousands of men including Michael's father Joe. His wife Katherine worked in a department store, giving them enough to buy a small house in the appropriately but coincidentally named Jackson Street.

Walking down the gravel path to the front of 2300 Jackson Street, it is impossible to imagine how eleven people lived inside. The house is tiny, literally the size of a large garage. There were two small bedrooms, a bathroom, living room and kitchen. This was the home of Michael, his parents Joe and Katherine, his brothers Jackie, Tito, Jermaine, Marlon and Randy and his sisters, Rebbie, LaToya and Janet. There was no arguing over who got which bedroom. Mum and Dad were in one, the boys in the second and the girls in the living room. Michael slept in a bunk bed with his brothers. Despite the cramped conditions, Michael's cousin Sheradon remembers the Jacksons as a happy bunch.

"The attitude of Michael and his family was, 'That's life.' They had to

*Roosevelt High School, scene of
The Jackson 5's triumphant victory in the
Gary citywide talent contest.*

*The aptly named street where the
Jackson family lived.*

*2300 Jackson Street. Michael's home until he left
Gary at the age of ten. Eleven people lived in the
tiny, two bedroomed house.*

make do the best way they could. Although there were nine brothers and sisters and Mum and Dad in just three rooms, they all got along really well."

The family might have been close but Joe and Katherine differed sharply in their attitude towards bringing up their children. Katherine showered them with love. She had had a hard life, plagued by polio which left her with a permanent limp. Katherine was a warm, generous, deeply religious person who taught the importance of honesty and kindness. Joe shared the same values but he had his own way of getting them across.

"His father was very strict", says Michael's cousin Annie. "I've heard about those stories of Michael and his brothers being beaten and I do know their Dad wouldn't tolerate any nonsense." Indeed the boys were beaten, Michael has spoken of his father hitting him with a belt, and while this might have made him behave, it was also the start of years of animosity between father and son.

The Jacksons were always a musical family. Katherine loved singing, and one of Michael's earliest memories is of his mother rocking him to sleep with her lullabies.

His father Joe had his own band, 'The Falcons' which used to play in clubs and colleges around Indiana. Joe Jackson's pride and joy was his electric guitar, kept in a closet at the house. The closet was strictly out of bounds for the children but when his dad was out at work, Tito would 'borrow' the guitar, sneak it into his bedroom and play along to his favourite songs on the radio. Eventually the inevitable happened and Tito broke a string on his father's precious instrument. When Joe found out, he was furious. He yelled at Tito who burst into tears and promised never to touch the guitar again. Joe Jackson was about to give his son a beating when a thought crossed his mind – a thought that probably changed the course of musical history. "O.K." he said, "If you're so good let's see what you can do." Tito picked up the guitar nervously and played some of the riffs and scales he had taught himself.

Joe was impressed. His son was a natural and it was not just Tito who was showing potential. Jackie and Jermaine joined in the jamming session and even Michael, two years old and barely able to walk, was bopping around happily.

The brothers were well pleased. Their father was clearly impressed. Maybe now they could borrow his guitar without asking. But Joe Jackson had greater things in mind. He had often dreamt of showbusiness success for himself and his band. That clearly was not to be, but he would now put all his time, energy and money into passing on that chance of glory to his children.

Tito, Jackie and Jermaine spent two years polishing their act before they were joined firstly by Marlon, then Michael, initially on bongos and eventually replacing Jermaine on vocals.

Michael's singing talents had not gone unnoticed in the Jacksons' neighbourhood. "He used to come over and play in the yard, climbing trees and going down to play in our basement with my brother," says neighbour Janine Bray. "He was always singing. All you had to do was offer him a piece of candy and he'd start to sing."

Another family friend, Lola Hayes, remembers Michael as a fun-loving boy.

"He was just like any other

Gary, Indiana. Town centre.

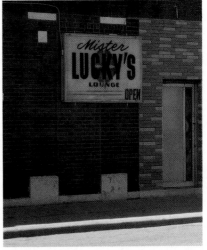

Mr Lucky's nightclub where The Jackson 5 had their first professional engagement.

playful child, running around having a good time, and every now and then he'd do a little dance. I remember him dancing and doing all those showbiz things when he was just four or five. Michael and his brothers never got into trouble. When they were not playing, the boys were kept very busy. Joe would make them do odd jobs around the house, then he would call them together to rehearse. There was always music coming out of that little house but none of the neighbours seemed to mind because it sounded so good."

It was good; Michael's father saw to that. A strict rehearsal schedule was drawn up with practise before and after school. Janine Bray often went over to the house to watch. "When Michael and his brothers rehearsed it sometimes became quite tense

because they wanted everything they did to be perfect. They'd go through songs over and over again until their voices blended perfectly with the music. Their father would make them perform for hours, from the moment they got back from school until late at night. If there was a concert coming up they could not run out and play like the rest of the children. Michael definitely had a sheltered childhood but he was happy because he did not know any other way to live."

Not only was Michael missing out on fun and games with children of his own age, he was also having to put up with the taunts of local schoolkids. They would gather outside the house when the brothers were rehearsing and yell, "You'll never make it." Rocks were even hurled through the windows. But the shouts of abuse

Michael's parents, Joe and Katherine Jackson.

just made the family more determined. They were going to make it and no amount of insults from jealous kids was going to stop them.

Michael's first memory of singing in front of an audience was at a school concert when he was five years old. He walked out onto the stage of Garnett Elementary School in Gary and sang 'Climb Ev'ry Mountain' from 'The Sound of Music'. The performance earned him a standing ovation and left his teachers with tears of emotion running down their faces. It was the shape of things to come.

Michael was no normal child, and that included his relationship with his teachers. He loved them so much that he stole jewellery from his mother to give to them as presents. He was never an academic genius but he did as he was told and managed to keep up with the work despite the pressure of

rehearsals. "Michael was a cute, good looking kid and he used to get most of the attention because he was the smallest," recalls Dolena Mack, who taught music at Garnett. "Michael was never really bad at school. He was shy and pretty reserved. Seeing him as a student in class you would never think he could explode like he did when he got up to sing. I guess performing just brought out another personality in him. When he sang it seemed like the music overtook him and nothing else mattered. Then when he finished he was just a normal school kid, back to being shy again. But as far as being a pupil was concerned, Michael was never any trouble."

By the time he was six years old, Michael Jackson was becoming a seasoned public performer. He and his brothers played talent shows at local schools and they virtually always won.

Family friend Raynard Jones

The Jackson 5: Jermaine, Jackie, Tito, Michael (second from right) and Marlon, with younger brother Randy at the back.

From his earliest performances, it was obvious that Michael was destined for great things.

played with the group at the most important talent show of them all; the citywide contest at Roosevelt High School. All of Gary's top performers would be battling for the coveted trophy. "Michael was frightened about the concert," says Raynard, "but we gave him a little reassurance and once he got out on stage he did a really great job. The crowd loved him and we won."

Nobody had ever seen anything like Michael Jackson. His brothers were good but he was amazing. "Music was his whole personality," says teacher Dolena Mack. "It wasn't just coming out of his voice. It was coming out of his hands, his feet...his whole body. Whenever you saw the Jacksons perform you could tell Michael would be the one to catch everybody's eye and go on to great things."

The brothers performed under various names. First they were known as 'The Ripples And Waves Plus Michael', then 'The Jackson Brothers' and eventually 'The Jackson 5'.

The group, with Michael singing, and his brothers on guitars, drums and background vocals, got their first paying concerts at a nightclub in Gary called Mr Lucky's. "We gave them two dollars a night and their little faces would light up when they got the money," says Celestine Williams who ran the club with her husband. "Michael might only have been seven or eight but when he got up on stage and did his little dances, everyone went wild. They'd cheer and throw money for him. Michael would go around picking up the coins and by the end of the evening his pockets would be bulging."

Because the boys were under age, they had to be smuggled in and out of the club through a side door. They played five shows, six nights a week. On the seventh their father would try to get them an appearance in Chicago. On top of all that, Michael and his brothers had to rehearse and do their schoolwork.

It was a gruelling schedule. Any hopes of a normal childhood for Michael had vanished. His friends were his brothers, his life was his music. But Michael would not have had it any other way. He was beginning to realise that he had a special talent. He was able to make a room full of strangers fall in love with him instantly, just by opening his mouth and moving his feet.

As Michael spun around the dancefloor of Mr Lucky's nightclub, thrilling the crowd with his versions of the James Brown and Motown hits, he dreamt of performing in front of tens of thousands of adoring fans who had all come to see The Jackson 5, the biggest band in the land!

He did not have long to wait.

2

ABC

The official record company version of events claimed that The Jackson 5 were discovered by Diana Ross when she saw them play in Gary. The story went that she was so impressed, she immediately got them signed to the world famous Motown record company and launched them on the road to fame and fortune.

This fairytale start to the group's career went down well with the fans. Unfortunately it was little more than a fairytale, conjured up by record company publicists with a vivid imagination.

Michael and his brothers had their first big break in 1968 when Gordon Keith, the owner of a small record company in Gary, signed them to his label. Steeltown Records aimed to give local bands a chance to make the big time, and when Gordon saw The Jackson 5 audition in their tiny living room, he had no doubts.

He hired a recording studio and every Saturday morning for the next few weeks the boys would go in and lay down tracks for their first record. Michael was fascinated by the studio. He wanted to know how everything worked and did not seem put off by the oversized

headphones which came halfway down his neck.

Michael would never forget the day when, just nine years old, he and his family gathered around the radio to hear The Jackson 5 blast out of the speakers for the first time. The single 'Big Boy' went into the top ten in Gary and was a minor hit in other cities.

As the boys got used to being local celebrities, the hard work continued. Their father stepped up rehearsals, although it was sometimes hard to keep the young lead singer in line.

"Michael's attention span wasn't too great," says friend and Jackson 5 musician Raynard Jones. The group would often use the basement of his larger house to rehearse.

"One day we were trying to get him to do a certain move and for some reason he was feeling a bit rebellious. He went over to the couch, picked up a little hammer and shouted, "I'm not going to do it." He hit the couch with the hammer and put a hole in it and that hole is still there today."

As word of The Jackson 5 and their amazing young singer spread, the brothers took their act further and further afield, winning talent shows in Indiana, Chicago and eventually New York. The big one was at the Apollo Theatre in New York which had become a Mecca for the new American black artists. James Brown, the Jacksons' hero, was a regular at the Apollo and to win talent night there in front of the toughest audience in the city was a virtual passport to success.

The Jackson 5 won and got a standing ovation.

The end of the 1960s was approaching. The world was looking for a group to replace The Beatles in their hearts and charts. The audience at the Apollo had just found them.

The Jackson 5 in one of their first official publicity shots. In the early days at Motown the group had a sixth member, Johnny Jackson.
◁

Berry Gordy, without doubt one of the most powerful men in the American music industry, sat at his desk in his luxurious Californian mansion, listening on the telephone to his excited colleague. One of his talent spotters had seen a group in Chicago. They were a bunch of kids, but one of the most talented and exciting live acts he had ever seen. Most amazing of all was the nine year old lead singer. Gordy was assured that this boy was phenomenal. He just had to be seen.

Thousands of miles away in Gary, Indiana, Michael Jackson was dashing home from school. That night they were due to leave for New York where they had been invited onto 'The David Frost Show' for their first national TV appearance.

Michael arrived at the house brimming over with excitement, only to be met by his father's stern face.

"The trip's off. I cancelled." Michael stared at his father in disbelief. How could he do this to them? Their first chance to appear on television across America.

Then Joe Jackson smiled. "Motown called," he said. "We've got an audition."

A chill ran down Michael's spine. After all the hours of rehearsing, the months spent perfecting his dance routines and the never ending circuit of clubs and talent shows, the moment he had been waiting for had finally arrived.

It is impossible to exaggerate the importance of the Motown record company, both the impact it made back in the sixties, and the influence that same music still has today.

Without Motown there would have been no Stevie Wonder, no Diana Ross or Lionel Richie and almost certainly no Michael Jackson. Stars from The Beatles to Madonna have spoken of how the Motown sound influenced them, while the likes of Phil Collins and Rod Stewart have honoured that sound by recording their own versions of Motown classics like 'You Can't Hurry Love' and 'This Old Heart of Mine'.

Under the ever watchful eye of its founder Berry Gordy, Motown pioneered the perfect pop song. Short sharp hits with catchy lyrics, brilliantly produced tunes and above all, exceptional performers.

Berry Gordy liked to encourage a family atmosphere at Motown, and until the end of the sixties, the main studio was located in a house in Detroit. (Detroit, the centre of America's car industry was known as 'motor town', hence the name 'Motown'.)

It was a warm July morning when the family van, with a huge 'Jackson 5' painted on the side, pulled up at the Motown house. Jackie, the eldest, was seventeen. Michael, the youngest, was nine. The brothers performed three songs in the famous studio and film of their performance was sent to Berry Gordy at his Los Angeles headquarters. Three days later The Jackson 5 were signed to Motown.

The family spent the first few months of their time at Motown living in Gary during the week and recording in Detroit at the weekend. At this stage, family friend Johnny Jackson (no relation) was also in the group. He was later made a backing musician before finally leaving the band.

In December 1968 the boys flew to Los Angeles to play at Berry Gordy's Christmas party. It was a day Michael Jackson would never forget.

"We went to his mansion. It had an indoor pool and all the Motown stars were there and they loved our show. Diana Ross came over to us after the concert. She kissed us all and said we were marvellous and that she wanted to play a special part in our career."

Michael was spellbound by Diana Ross. Here was one of the world's greatest entertainers, telling him how good he was!

For her part, Diana adored Michael. He was cute and shy but above all amazingly talented. She could tell immediately that he was destined for superstardom and was only too happy to give him all the advice and support that she could.

Their friendship blossomed a few months later when the brothers finally moved to Los Angeles, which had become Motown's new base. Michael's mother was staying in Gary for the time being to look after fourteen year old LaToya and Janet, aged four. LaToya was taking care of the boys' fan mail while Janet was desperately trying to prove that she could sing as well as her brothers.

Berry Gordy decided that Michael should move into Diana Ross's home. Diana was delighted. Michael could not believe his luck: "Berry lived at the top of the hill and Diana lived just a block away. Being there was a big thrill."

In the studio the boys got to work on their first Motown single 'I Want You Back'. There was no problem getting Michael to sing but he did need some help reaching the microphone. "I had my own little apple box I had to stand on because I couldn't reach. It even had my name written on it."

The Motown philosophy was simple. Every song had to be perfect or it would not be released. The record company's producers were taking no risks with The Jackson 5's first single. They made Michael record the song over and over again, until they were completely satisfied.

'I Want You Back' was released in October 1969. It steadily climbed the charts and on 31 January 1970 it hit the number one spot in America, going on to sell six million copies.

Overnight, Michael and his brothers had become America's hottest act. Every TV and radio show in the country wanted them as guests. Wherever they went they were mobbed by adoring fans. 'Jacksonmania' spread like wildfire. Posters of the brothers decorated millions of bedroom walls, while fans decorated themselves in Jackson 5 T-shirts, earrings and buttons.

The success meant that Michael's mother and the rest of the family could finally leave the small house in Gary and join the boys in California.

They bought a house in Los Angeles which was immediately besieged by fans desperate for a glimpse of their heroes. Security guards were put on the gates and the family's telephone number had to be changed every month.

'I Want You Back' was followed by the release of the group's first album, 'Diana Ross Presents The Jackson 5'. Motown did all they could to push the story that Diana Ross had discovered the band. Michael and the brothers happily recited the story in dozens of interviews.

The Jackson 5's public image was carefully orchestrated by the record company. They were given new haircuts and new clothes, as well as lessons in dancing, singing and grammar. Staff from Motown would conduct mock interviews with the boys, who were given precise instructions on how to answer questions from journalists.

The next single was 'ABC', to this day one of Michael's favourites. In many ways it is the ultimate pop song. Using much the same tune as 'I Want You Back', it had the simplest lyrics imaginable, but once people heard the song, they could not stop singing it.

'ABC' knocked The Beatles off the number one spot in February 1970. Three months later the third single, 'The Love You Save' did the same thing, and in August, as Michael approached his twelfth birthday, The Jackson 5's first ballad 'I'll Be There' got to number one where it stayed for five weeks.

Two years earlier, Berry Gordy had sat down with the boys and made them a promise.

"I'm gonna make you the biggest thing in the world. Your first record will be a number one, your second record will be a number one and so will your third."

The Motown supremo had exceeded even his high expectations. The Jackson 5's first four singles had all reached the top of the charts, the best start any group had ever had.

For Michael, these were the happiest days of his life. For much of the time he was looked after by Berry Gordy's sister Esther who was Motown's vice president.

"When Michael was a little boy he was always very happy. He couldn't stand still. He was always moving, dancing and singing or if there were lots of people around he'd just mime his songs."

Michael certainly had a lot to sing and dance about.

Apart from being the lead singer of the world's most popular group, he was living a life he had only dreamt about back in Gary. Compared to his home town, California was paradise; palm trees, long sandy beaches, fabulous shops, and the place that was virtually to become his second home...Disneyland.

By the end of his first trip to Disneyland, Michael was captivated by this magical kingdom, where the harsh realities of the outside world were replaced with adventure, happiness and love.

He would spend hours playing around the Disneyland streets with his brothers and squealing with

Michael soon adapted to the luxuries of the family's new Californian lifestyle.

On the crest of a wave. Performing one of the early hits on a Jackson 5 TV special.

▷

16

delight when he spotted Donald Duck or Mickey Mouse. These early visits made a lasting impression on Michael.

"I just eat it up. In Disneyland you forget about the rest of the world. When you walk down Main Street you just feel so good. It's real escapism."

A budding artist, Michael's bedroom was covered with cartoons he had drawn of his favourite Disney characters, and he had copies of all the Walt Disney movies.

Michael's love of animals also developed during his early days in California. While his brothers were out playing sport or partying, Michael would spend hours with his animals in the yard; dogs, cats, rabbits, he loved them all. At a photo session on Santa Monica beach, he even caught a snake and took it home to join the collection.

When Michael first arrived in California he went to the local school and tried to get involved as best he could, but deep down he was just not interested.

During lessons he would sit in class drawing and daydreaming. When a teacher asked a question he usually had not been paying attention and did not know the answer, but he did not care. By his early teens a tough determination was developing under that softly spoken, shy exterior. He would never boast but he knew full well that it was his talent and pulling power that had taken The Jackson 5 to the top. He had been studying showbusiness for as long as he could remember and was learning something new every day. He would carry on studying, practising and perfecting his performance until he could out-dance and out-perform every entertainer on the planet. Michael kept up with his classwork to keep his parents happy but school was, quite simply, irrelevant.

In fact, when Michael speaks of his education now, he speaks of only one place; Motown.

"Going through that whole thing was just the greatest learning point. I learnt about producing. I learnt how to cut a track. I learnt how to write. Just being at sessions with people like Stevie Wonder was incredible. It was the best school I could ever wish for."

Michael would fool around like any other youngster. One of his favourite pranks was sticking silly labels on the producers' backs without them knowing. Yet what set him apart from his brothers was his thirst for knowledge. In the studio he wanted to know what everyone was doing and why. By his teens, Michael had a thorough knowledge of studio operations. Often he would sit quietly in the control room, just watching and learning.

The greatest thing that Michael learnt from Motown was the art of perfection. It was never enough for a song to be good, it had to be the best. Every single note had to have 100 per cent effort put into it and if there were any doubts about a song, it was scrapped.

This perfectionism was to become a virtual obsession later in his career, but the results were to prove astounding.

O nce The Jackson 5 hit the top of the charts, it was time for the fans to see them in person. As the boys began their first tour, the full extent of 'Jacksonmania' became apparent. When they flew into Philadelphia for a concert in May 1970 there were three and a half thousand screaming fans waiting to greet them at the airport.

Michael was eleven years old

and terrified.

Hundreds of hysterical girls broke through the airport barriers with one thing in mind: they all wanted a piece of Michael Jackson.

As he tried to fight his way through the crowd, all he could hear was screaming, all he could see were dozens of grabbing hands. The security guards eventually got to the boys and whisked them away to their hotel. Michael was in tears. His security advisor sat him down and gave him what tips he could on coping with crowd hysteria, the main one being to shield his eyes with his hands to stop girls' finger nails causing some nasty damage. It was another lesson that was to stay with Michael for the rest of his life.

The scenes of hysteria were repeated at the concert in Philadelphia. More than a hundred police were needed to stop fans storming the stage. Within seconds of the boys finishing their final number they were rushed through the stage door into limousines and back to the hotel under police escort.

If the American fans were wild, the English ones were crazy. Ten thousand were waiting at the airport when The Jackson 5 arrived in London on their 1972 European tour.

At the band's hotel, police had to use water hoses to stop hysterical girls blocking the road.

The highlight of the trip to England was a Royal Command Performance in front of the Queen.

"I'd read all these things in my schoolbooks about England and the Queen, but after we did the Royal Command Performance, there I was actually looking into her eyes. It was the greatest thing in the world."

Michael's father Joe remained the group's manager. This meant that he was always on tour with the boys. It also meant they had to behave themselves. They might have been the most successful band in the land but it was still lights out at 11pm for The Jackson 5.

That did not stop the boys getting up to their fair share of pranks. Michael and his brothers came up with their own under age version of rock'n'roll rebellion.

There were no wild parties or TV sets thrown through hotel windows. Instead the boys would fill paper bags with water and drop them out of windows on unsuspecting passers by.

Pillow fights were also a favourite, while buckets filled with water would often be delicately balanced on top of bedroom doors ready to soak the next brother to walk in.

Michael was a great practical joker and would collapse in fits of laughter if he ever caught anyone out.

In hotels, his particular favourite was to phone room service, order the most expensive meal on the menu and get it delivered to someone else's room, together with the bill.

The press would always try to look for rivalry between the brothers, but at this stage their success actually brought them closer together. They did not mix with other children and made few friends, which meant that they had to rely on each other for companionship.

"There was no rivalry between us," says Jermaine. "Our father was very strict and he wouldn't allow any in-fighting."

Younger sister LaToya also remembers the boys being very close in the early days. "They were constantly giving each other help and information. Our parents taught us not to be envious or jealous, but proud of each other."

Nevertheless, it did not require a degree in music to tell who the star of the group was. Just listening to songs like 'ABC' showed how Michael carried the brothers along. He was not showing off, he simply shone with talent.

Michael's solo career began at the age of thirteen. There was no question at this stage of him leaving the group, but the time had come to test his popularity, away from the rest of the family.

"That was Berry Gordy's idea. He thought I should spin out and do different things, different kinds of music so I wasn't obligated to one sound."

The first solo single was the soulful ballad 'Got To Be There,' released in October 1971. It sold one and a half million copies, just missing the number one spot.

Michael was back in more playful mood for 'Rockin' Robin'. The critics dismissed it as meaningless pop, but Michael did not care and neither did the fans. They bought it in their hundreds of thousands and 'Rockin' Robin' made number two.

In the end though, it was to be a song on the bizarre subject of rats that gave Michael his first solo number one. 'Ben' was the soundtrack to a film about a boy who befriended a rat. Not everyone's ideal choice for a movie, but for Michael it combined beautifully his love of children's stories with his fondness for animals. Michael was also singing from experience. In building what was rapidly becoming his own personal zoo, he had tried his hand as a rat breeder. He managed to buy a collection of rats and put them in a lovingly prepared cage. They promptly ate each other. This proved too much even for Michael's Dr Doolittle instincts. The rats that were left were sent back.

Apart from topping the charts, 'Ben' was also significant because it was Michael Jackson's first serious involvement in the world of films. He would go to see the movie over and over again just to hear his song and see his name on the screen. It was a dream come true for the young movie lover who would spend days closeted in his room losing himself in the magic of the old classic films. Now he was beginning to realise that his musical talents could help to make him a Hollywood star. It was an opportunity not to be missed.

Even though 'Ben' reached number one in America, many radio stations thought a love song to a rat was just too ridiculous and refused to play it. Once again, the experts were out of touch with the fans. The song immediately became a firm favourite. "Wherever we went, the whole world demanded to hear it" says Michael. "We couldn't get off stage without people chanting for 'Ben'..."

Saturday morning was, without doubt, the highlight of young Michael Jackson's week. He would jump out of bed, switch the television on, and join millions of children across America to watch 'The Jackson 5 Cartoon Show'. While most pop stars yearn for top selling records and prestigious awards, having a cartoon show based on his own life story was the greatest tribute Michael could wish for.

Unlike the average thirteen year old, who was growing out of Walt Disney, fairy stories and cartoons, Michael was becoming more absorbed by them every day.

His love of childlike things has

Away from his brothers
Michael began to establish his solo career.

21

always made him the brunt of jokes and cruel comments but Michael Jackson has never been and never will be interested in the wild side of the rock 'n' roll lifestyle. This can be traced back to his intense religious upbringing.

Michael's mother was a Jehovah's Witness. One of the strictest religions there is, the Witnesses believe that when the world ends, only a limited few, the good and pure, will go to heaven. Michael took this very seriously. He loved his mother, he loved his family, he loved his music, his cartoons and his animals. As long as he could go through life being good and making people happy, then he was happy.

He also did not have the problem of friends leading him astray. Michael had few, if any close friends. The brothers enjoyed their own company. People 'outside' only seemed interested in getting to know them because they were famous. Michael did not go to school, the fans had made that impossible, and he now had his own private tutor.

Quite simply, Michael Jackson was beginning to build his own fantasy world away from anything that resembled normality. He could lose himself in the wonders of Disneyland whenever he wished. He could watch any movie he wanted in his own private screening room, and now, to top it all, he was a cartoon!

What more could a thirteen year old boy ask for?

The Jackson 5 spent much of 1971 and 1972 touring. They had a massive following who had been desperate to see them since the early hits.

The concerts were a spectacular success but despite the tens of thousands of screaming fans, The Jackson 5 had reached their peak.

'I'll Be There' had turned out to be their last number one back in 1970. The next two singles, 'Mama's Pearl' and 'Never Can Say Goodbye' got to number two, 'Sugar Daddy' in 1972 reached number ten, but the next few singles were only minor hits.

Michael's solo career also took a nosedive after 'Ben,' with some of his records not even making the charts.

It was not that Michael and the group were no longer good. Technically, their singing, playing and performing were improving all the time, but the novelty of The Jackson 5 was beginning to wear off on the fans. The brothers no longer just wanted to perform light and fluffy pop songs like 'I Want You Back' and 'ABC'. Unfortunately, their new material did not appeal so much to the younger end of the audience and often did not impress the older fans either.

To make matter worse, The Jackson 5's lead singer was no longer a cute little ten year old with a cheeky grin. Michael Jackson was growing up and he was not enjoying it.

Firstly, at the age of fourteen he shot up in height. Fans would go into a room looking for Michael Jackson and walk straight past, not recognising him.

When they did meet him, they often seemed disappointed that he was no longer the cuddly kid they had been expecting.

Michael could just about cope with that, but the second obvious sign of his adolescence caused him much worse problems…He was getting spots.

Michael is quoted as saying that his spots messed up his whole personality. Everyone knows how embarrassing they can be but for Michael, who was shy at the best of times, they were unbearable. Not only did he have to put up with jokes from his brothers, he also had to share his ugly zits with millions who saw him in magazines and on television. Michael responded to the embarrassment by cutting himself

off from the outside world.

He did not want to see anyone and when he did meet people he would not look them in the eye. If he had the choice of staying in or going out, he would always choose to shut himself in his room with a good book or an old movie.

On top of that he felt guilty. The group depended on him for their success but they were not having hits. As far as Michael was concerned, the lack of success was his fault. Add to that the fact that his voice was breaking, and all thoughts of the future filled him with fear.

This pressure was a terrible burden for Michael. Because he was the focal point of the group, he felt directly responsible for his brothers. In many ways he was, and this was to prove a major problem in the years to come.

It was not just Michael who was unhappy. All of the brothers realised that The Jackson 5 were reaching crisis point. The fans who had bought 'ABC' were growing up and their musical tastes were changing. If the group could not change and develop with them, they would be cast aside and quickly become musical history.

The family blamed Motown for the lack of hits. When The Jackson 5 were first signed up, Berry Gordy and his team took responsibility for everything. They wrote the songs, they produced the records, they decided what the boys should wear, what they should say and where they should go. The group was a carefully cultivated product and the boys did as they were told. That was fine in the early days, but as time went by they grew more and more frustrated.

By 1975, Michael and his brothers had been making music for ten years, yet they were still not

Underneath the smiles, all was not well in the Jackson family.

allowed to write or produce their own songs. The record company dictated everything and Michael in particular felt that his talents were not being used to the full.

"A lot of times I found it frustrating. I had a couple of disputes with Motown producers. One time the producer wanted me to pronounce words a certain way, and I told him that if you pronounce the words so precisely it takes away from the feeling of the song. In the end I was right and I won."

The group was also unhappy about its finances. They were still on a very low royalty rate and the record company controlled all their publishing rights, depriving them of a valuable source of income.

As tension increased between the Jackson family and Motown, the pressure grew on their father Joe to confront Berry Gordy. But while everyone debated what to do, sixteen year old Michael came to a decision. He was the undoubted leader of the group, he still regarded Berry Gordy as a father figure... he would speak to him on behalf of the family.

Without his father or brothers knowing, Michael called Gordy and arranged a meeting. The quiet, shy teenager walked into Gordy's office and sat down.

"We're unhappy at Motown, Berry. Do you want us to leave or what?" Berry Gordy, used to the superficial charm of many showbiz stars was surprised at Michael's directness. They spoke for half an hour. Gordy explained that he did not think the boys were ready to take greater control of their careers. Michael explained patiently that they were.

They parted without reaching agreement.

The meeting was a turning point for Michael, partly because it decided the family's future, but even more significantly, Michael had begun to take his career into his own hands.

After a decade in the music industry, he had a sound business head on his young shoulders. He had been careful to observe how the music industry worked. He was fascinated at the way Berry Gordy controlled such a huge musical empire. He also watched his father manage the group and took careful note of his good and bad decisions. He might only have been sixteen, but Michael had a clear picture of his and his brothers' potential, both musically and financially.

His parents and brothers were surprised and annoyed at Michael for meeting Gordy on his own, but as they would soon realise, his determination and business abilities were things they would have to learn to live with.

The family gathered for a meeting in one of the huge rooms at their mansion in Encino, California, as they did whenever an important decision had to be made.

The routine was well established. They would discuss the problem and then vote on it. Everyone had an equal say.

The choice was clear. They could stay at Motown, or they could take up one of the offers from the many record companies willing to give them more money and more independence.

When the vote came, everyone raised their hands. The verdict was unanimous. The Motown days were over.

3

IN BETWEEN DAYS

The best offer came from CBS. Regarded as one of the giants in the music industry, the record company already had an up and coming star called Bruce Springsteen, and was keen to sign more artists.

Songs like 'Dancing Machine' had convinced the company's bosses that Motown was not making the most of The Jackson 5. The disco craze was sweeping America and if anyone could make hot dance records, the Jackson brothers could.

The group signed to Epic records, part of the CBS empire, for a reported advance of 750 thousand dollars. Their royalty fee was substantially higher than it had been at Motown and the group was promised much greater involvement in the production of its records.

Everything should have been set for a wonderful re-launch of their career, but it was not to be. Breaking away from Motown turned out to be a long and very painful affair.

The main problem was Jermaine. In 1973 Michael's older brother had married Berry Gordy's daughter Hazel.

When the group left Motown,

Jermaine was torn between loyalty to his family and his wife. In the end he chose Hazel.

"The public and press were trying to come between us saying I'd disowned my family, but it wasn't true. It was just a matter of business."

Jermaine refused to sign the contract with CBS, and following a phone call from Berry Gordy, he walked out on The Jackson 5 half an hour before one of their concerts.

There had been some vicious family rows between Jermaine and his brothers, with Michael desperately trying to keep the peace and not take sides.

"I would say that was the most tense situation ever," says Michael. "I was in a whole new world, there was so much tension and I just wasn't sure what was going to happen."

In the end, the group just went on without Jermaine, and Randy took his place.

Michael was shocked at the actions of the Motown boss in persuading his brother to leave the band, but when it came to business, Berry Gordy was ruthless, and he was not through yet.

When The Jackson 5 joined Motown in 1968 they signed away all rights to the group's name. In effect Berry Gordy owned a copyright on the name, and now that they had left his label he was not going to let them carry on using it. Gordy's lawyer phoned Joe Jackson. He made it quite clear that if they carried on calling themselves 'The Jackson 5', Motown would sue.

The brothers and their father were furious, yet Michael could not help but be impressed at Gordy's sharp business sense. The group had paid the price for not getting the right legal advice. The Motown school had taught Michael Jackson a final, important lesson.

Now forced to call themselves 'The Jacksons', the first album on CBS was also called 'The Jacksons'. It produced one major hit, 'Enjoy Yourself'. Before recording started, the brothers had embarked on their own TV series. Michael hated making the shows. He did not enjoy TV work because it did not leave him enough time to rehearse. Ever the perfectionist, he tried to convince his brothers to pull out of the shows, but they ignored him.

The next L.P. 'Goin' Places' in 1977 could only scrape up to number 63 in the album chart. Once again the group felt that their record company was holding them back. They were being allowed to have their say but most of the writing and production was out of their hands.

Despite their lack of success in the charts, The Jacksons still had a massive following. The fans did not share Michael's pre-occupation with his spots, and the tall eighteen year old with his bushy afro hair was becoming quite a sex symbol. When Michael went to a store in Memphis to sign records in 1977, ten

thousand fans turned up and he had to climb onto the roof to escape.

Interviewers often asked Michael about girlfriends. This was a typical answer to a question from journalist Timothy White:

TIMOTHY: "Do you have any girldfriends?"

MICHAEL: "I'm too busy for dating and girls right now. I'd like to try, maybe. What do you think? Think I should? Well I'll think about

that. We'll see... But I'm happy."

Michael's relationships with women have always been the subject of intense interest and speculation. Nobody knows for sure how many girlfriends he has had or what sort of relationships he has had with them. Michael Jackson's love life is by far his best kept secret.

During his early teenage years, it seems that Michael did not have any girlfriends. There are various stories told about the sexual exploits of the Jackson family on tour. His older brothers certainly made the most of the eager groupies. Marlon has said that he and Michael had to pretend to be asleep when Jermaine brought girls into the room at night.

Their father Joe also gained a reputation for womanising, something that disgusted Michael, who was angry at the way Joe was treating his mother.

It has been said that the rest of his family's casual approach to women appalled Michael, and ended any possibility of him succumbing to tempting offers from his adoring fans.

That could well be true, but

Not allowed to call themselves 'The Jackson 5',
the brothers entered the new era in their careers as 'The Jacksons.'
From left to right: Marlon, Jackie, Michael, Randy and Tito.

◁

more to the point, his religious beliefs would not permit sexual relationships outside marriage. He was also under the constantly watchful eye of his father and the record company minders. A scandal involving America's cleanest living young pop star could have had disastrous consequences for the group's image.

Girls were occasionally introduced to Michael on tour. Life on the road could be lonely and he enjoyed their company, but any teenager looking forward to a night of passion with their idol ended up very disappointed. Michael would sit and talk with them about anything from music to the bible but as for forming meaningful relationships, that was virtually impossible.

At home, Michael's parents continued to keep him closeted from the outside world. On tour, the constant round of hotels, airports and concerts left little time for starting long term friendships.

Michael's first serious girlfriend was Tatum O'Neal. Another child star, Tatum was the daughter of actor Ryan O'Neal. She had won her first Oscar at the age of nine and her fame spread with films like 'International Velvet'.

She and Michael became friends when he was nineteen and she was thirteen. Michael remembers sitting at the table of a club in Los Angeles when he felt a soft hand take hold of his. It took him by surprise. He was used to grabbing hands trying to pull off a piece of his hair but Tatum's gentle touch was different. They talked, immediately hit it off and exchanged phone numbers. Tatum invited Michael to a party at the famous Playboy mansion where they ended up in a hot tub together, although Michael insists to this day that they kept their bathing suits on.

The pair remained good friends for about two years. It is hard to say how serious they were about each other. Michael has said that they were in love, although Tatum

has given the impression that they were just close friends who enjoyed each other's company.

Michael has always been the subject of rumours which have hurt him deeply. Around this time, word spread like wildfire that he was going to have a sex change operation. The first Michael knew of his impending transformation into a woman was when a tearful girl came up to him in a store.

"Michael, tell me it's not true, please."

"What?" asked Michael, upset

to see the fan sobbing.

"They're saying you're going to have an operation to become a woman."

Michael could not believe his ears, but the girl even told him that she had read about it in her favourite magazine.

"It's absolutely untrue," he said. "Now go and tell all your friends and stop worrying."

Michael put on a brave face but he felt like bursting into tears. Here he was, a young man just making music and trying to make people happy. Why would anybody want to upset him by spreading these vicious lies?

What hurt him most were the rumours that he was gay.

He would go to his mother in tears when he read the nasty stories

in the papers. The press just could not accept that he was happy playing music and living at home surrounded by the family and pets he loved. Because he was not out womanising every night, something had to be wrong.

One day a reporter asked him:

"Are you, or are you not gay?"

"No," replied Michael. "I am not gay. I am not homo. Not at all. People make up stories about me being gay because they have nothing else to do. I'm not going to let it get to me. I'm not going to have a nervous breakdown because people think I'm having sex with men. I'm sure I must have lots of fans who are gay and I don't mind that. That's their life and this is mine."

Journalists were quick to catch onto the fact that he was rarely seen in the company of women, but what they failed to appreciate was Michael's strict upbringing. The Jehovah's Witness faith forbids casual relationships. It actually forbids relationships with anyone who is not a fellow Witness, and dating is only something that happens before marriage.

The older brothers were not concerned about that, but Michael remained a devout follower of the faith. Serious dating and marriage were for the future.

Apart from anything else, what Michael saw of marriage did not impress him. By the mid 1970s his brothers Jermaine, Jackie, Marlon and Tito had all married and at various stages all seemed to be going through problems. Jermaine's marriage to Hazel Gordy had split the family and at one stage Jackie filed for divorce, before eventually getting back with his wife.

There were also rumours of affairs, not least involving his own father, whose casual attitude towards his mother continued to upset Michael deeply.

All in all, Michael Jackson could think of far better things to do with his time than get involved with women.

In July 1977, Michael was playing in the sea at Jermaine's beachside home when he felt a sharp pain in his chest. It was unbearable and he could hardly breathe.

Gasping, he stumbled back through the sand to the house. Jermaine called an ambulance and Michael was rushed to hospital in agony.

Doctors calmed Michael down telling him that a blood vessel had burst in his lung but that everything was going to be alright.

Once he had recovered, one of the senior doctors went into his room for a quiet word. He was concerned that Michael was overworking, pushing himself too hard to try to please his family.

Michael smiled and thanked the doctor for his concern. He promised that he would try to take things easier.

The medical staff were wasting their words. Writing songs, working day and night in the studio and touring the world did not strike Michael as particularly hard work. It was his life and nothing could stop his never ending quest for success.

Some of those close to Michael

have claimed that he has suffered similar attacks over the years which have been hushed up to avoid scaring the fans. As any doctor will confirm, working hard and striving for perfection is fine, but if it is taken too far, a person's health will inevitably be affected.

By the time he was eighteen, Michael still had one big unfulfilled ambition... He wanted to be a film star. He had spent his teens watching hundreds of films and would play his favourites over and over again, observing how all the great actors worked and imagining him in their place.

Until now, it had been hard for him to pursue his ambition. He was far too busy with his brothers, and his father did not like the idea of him breaking away and doing his own thing. But when movie director Sidney Lumet called Michael and asked him to star in a remake of 'The Wizard of Oz', he could not refuse.

'The Wiz' was to be an updated, black musical version of the children's classic.

Michael was to be the scarecrow and Diana Ross was to play Dorothy.

Michael could not contain his excitement. He had seen 'The Wizard of Oz' on Broadway at least six times and cried at every show. In the weeks before filming he would run around the house doing his scarecrow impersonations and practising the script.

The rest of the family did not share Michael's enthusiasm. His brothers and father joked about the film and told him that he would not be up to it. They were probably jealous. They were certainly worried. Michael was approaching the age when none of them would be able

to stop him doing as he pleased, yet their livelihoods depended on him staying with The Jacksons.

Michael had to move to New York for filming. Apart from touring, it was his first time away from home. He did not fancy being in the Big Apple on his own so he took LaToya with him, and they moved into a smart Manhattan apartment.

Michael loved his new found freedom and made the most of the New York nightlife. He would rehearse and film during the day, go clubbing at night and take in the sights with LaToya on his days off.

Michael leapt into his role as the scarecrow with total enthusiasm.

He became so absorbed in his character, he would often refuse to take the costume and make-up off once filming had finished. For those few precious hours every day he no longer had to cope with the pressures of being Michael Jackson. LaToya, who went along to watch the filming, would leave home in the morning with her brother and go home in the evening with a scarecrow. For Michael, it was another chance to live in a world of fantasy.

"I look out the back windows of cars and kids see me dressed up as the scarecrow. They get frightened because they don't know who or what it is. Sometimes when I come home with my make-up I keep dancing in front of the mirrors as the scarecrow. I forget everything else but the scarecrow's world. It's a feeling of peace and magic."

Michael loved every minute of his time in New York. Friends had never seen him so relaxed. For the first time in his life he could do exactly as he wanted. On the film set he only had to answer to the director. He did not have his brothers and a roomful of producers

telling him what to do.

Off the set, his time was his own. Michael mixed happily with his fellow stars and was easy going and chatty when he met fans.

He flew back to California in 1978, happier than ever. He treated himself to a Rolls-Royce for his twentieth birthday and after constant pressure from his parents, started learning to drive.

When 'The Wiz' was released, the critics hated it and it was a complete flop.

The producers and directors came in for heavy criticism, and most people agreed that Diana Ross was too old to play Dorothy. But among all the harsh words, one character was universally praised. Everyone agreed that the scarecrow was tremendous. His dancing and singing had been superb and if this was anything to go by, Michael Jackson's acting career was set to be long and spectacular.

Once they got him back home, Michael's brothers were keen to start work on the next album. The Jacksons' career was in the doldrums again and they desperately needed some hits.

Michael agreed, but before they could go back in the studio, one thing had to be sorted out once and for all.

He and his brothers were now adults. Between them, their musical and songwriting abilities were immense, yet they were still not being allowed to have full control of

their music.

The record company insisted on choosing most of the songs and producers, none of which were putting The Jacksons back at the top of the charts.

Michael and his father went to see CBS chief Ron Alexenburg and made their position clear. The record company was doing its best but it was not good enough. Either they be allowed to control the next album or they would consider leaving the record company.

What Michael and Joe did not know was that CBS was also having serious doubts and had virtually decided to drop The Jacksons. Luckily, one of the company's senior executives, Bobby Colomby, persuaded them to give the group one more chance.

Bobby, who got on well with all the family and was particularly fond of Michael, believed that the group was still destined for great things. He could see that Michael was brimming with ideas and should be held back no longer.

It was decided that he would oversee the album but that the group would be allowed to write and produce most of the songs.

The result was 'Destiny'. Ten years after signing with Motown, The Jacksons had finally written and produced their own album.

Finally in full control of the music, Michael was unable to hide his excitement in the studio. When he was recording 'Blame It On The Boogie', he suddenly ran out of the studio into the hall. His worried brothers dashed out to find him dancing and spinning around the floor.

"Sorry," said Michael, still boogying away. "I just want to dance but I didn't have enough room."

'Shake Your Body (Down To The

Ground)' was the big hit off the album. It was written by Michael and his brother Randy, got to number seven in America and sold two million copies. After years of battling with record company executives to let him prove what he was capable of, Michael had finally won.

"We went through so much with people not believing in us. They'd say, 'Are you sure you can do it?' and we'd say, 'Yes, we're sure,' and they'd say, 'Are you really sure?' and we'd say, 'We know we can, we know what we can do'. Then we went in and wrote the 'Destiny' album and it went double platinum. We were really happy and CBS thought it was great too."

While the album was a success for Michael, the tour that followed was certainly not. He lost his voice, and for many of the shows he had to mime while Marlon took over on lead vocals. His throat problems eventually became so bad, doctors forced him to cancel two weeks of concerts.

The family was worried. Michael's health troubles were just a symptom of his state of mind. He had become irritable, argumentative and at times, totally uninterested in what was going on around him.

When the 'Destiny' tour finished, Michael would lock himself away in his room for days and only appear for meals. He stopped turning up for family meetings and constantly seemed tired and depressed.

The problem was simple: the solution was not. Michael was battling with his conscience and it was ruining his life.

He was now almost 21 and it was time to make some difficult choices. He loved his brothers dearly but there were times when working within the group made him feel like a caged animal fighting to break free.

As long as he remained part of The Jacksons he would be restricted by the rest of the family. The group was very democratic. Everyone had their say and if there was a dispute they would take a vote on it.

Michael had reached the stage where he found this process infuriating. On many occasions in and out of the studio, he had to compromise on what he believed in, just to please the family. He realised that during the recording of 'Destiny' he had several great ideas that he had just let go because it was too much hassle trying to get his brothers interested.

His instincts told him that he had to break free. Yet he still felt responsible for the family. They depended on him, how could he let them down?

Eventually, Michael summoned up his courage and called a family meeting. He was not going to leave the group but he had decided to record a solo album. The brothers offered to help but Michael was firm:

"Sorry everyone . . . but I'm doing this one on my own."

The rest of the family mumbled their displeasure but they were powerless and they knew it.

His father seemed unconcerned.

"If he wants to record a solo album, let him. He made his own albums on Motown and they never did much."

Joe had a point. After a spectacular start, Michael's solo career had faded and his records had sold badly.

But as far as Michael was concerned, the situation now was completely different. He was older, more experienced and had many more ideas.

CBS had also promised him complete control over the album. They even let him choose his own producer . . . Quincy Jones.

Michael had become friends with Quincy while he was filming 'The Wiz'.

Quincy was the film's musical director and he has fond memories of their first meeting.

"During rehearsals there was a line where Michael had to say the name 'Socrates' and for three days he kept saying it wrong. He'd pronounce it 'So crea tees'. So on the third day I took him aside and said 'Michael, it's Socrates'. He looked up with those big eyes and that was the moment we bonded."

Michael hit it off with Quincy immediately.

"We really got to know each other on 'The Wiz' and we worked beautifully together, oh so well. I called him up one day and said, 'Quincy, I'm ready to do an album, a solo album. I've written the songs but I want a really good producer. I'm going to produce it too but I want someone to work with me'. I said, 'Can you recommend somebody?' and I wasn't trying to hint at all, I really wasn't, and he said, 'Smelly, why don't you let me do it?' and I started giggling and said, 'That's a great idea,' and that's how 'Off The Wall' came about."

As for the nickname, there are various versions of why Quincy chose to call him 'Smelly', the most likely being Michael's ability to sniff out a good deal. For his part, Michael just called his producer 'Q'.

In many ways, Quincy Jones seemed a strange choice to produce what was being regarded as Michael Jackson's make or break solo album. He had to prove himself to his family, his record company and the fans, yet the producer he wanted was best known for his jazz work and film soundtracks.

Nevertheless, when CBS expressed their doubts, Michael

remained defiant, and was to be proved totally right. His faith in Quincy Jones led to the most successful producer/performer relationship since George Martin and The Beatles.

On their first day in the studio Michael told Quincy what he wanted. He was still not sure exactly how the album should sound but he was sure of one thing. It had to be completely different from The Jacksons' albums.

Quincy admits that when they first went into the studio he had his doubts about the project. He found Michael "shy, introverted and non-assertive." But after a couple of sessions, that changed completely.

Quincy was just what Michael needed. He used his immense musical talents and years of production experience to the full, but he also encouraged Michael to push his ideas to the limit. They were the perfect combination.

When the time came to release the first single, Michael waited nervously for news on the song's performance in the charts. 'Don't Stop 'Til You Get Enough' was an irresistibly funky number written by Michael. He had come up with the melody while walking around the house, and the family soon became used to him singing the catchy chorus, although his mother had her doubts about the title.

Mrs Jackson's concerns were not shared by the fans. Within days of its release, 'Don't Stop 'Til You Get Enough' was the most played record on the radio. The follow up single, 'Off The Wall', made it into the top ten as did 'She's Out Of My Life', without doubt one of Michael's most moving ballads. Whatever his experiences of love, he sang the song with an emotion and depth of feeling that tugged the heartstrings of the most hardened

listeners.

Michael has always found recording love songs a deeply emotional experience. The lights in the studio are dimmed and a curtain is often drawn around him so that he is completely on his own.

At the very end of 'She's Out Of My Life', Michael's voice appears to crack with emotion. Greg Phillinganes was musical director for the 'Off The Wall' album. "When we recorded 'She's Out Of My Life', Michael got to the end of the song and started crying. He was so emotional he couldn't stop. It wasn't staged or anything like that. There's a lot of emotion in that song and Michael just felt the emotion."

Although he was now being allowed to write his own songs, Michael was still happy to use the talents of some of the world's great songwriters. Indeed, he only wrote three of 'Off The Wall's' ten tracks: 'Don't Stop 'Til You Get Enough', 'Working Day And Night' and 'Get On The Floor'.

For 'Off The Wall', 'Rock With You' and 'Burn This Disco Out', Quincy Jones brought in Rod Temperton, best known as the keyboard player with the British band Heatwave, who had a big hit with 'Boogie Nights'.

'I Can't Help It' was a Stevie Wonder song and 'Girlfriend' had been written especially for Michael by Paul McCartney.

Michael and Paul had first met at a party in Los Angeles. They shook hands and Paul said, "Hello, I've written a song for you."

The former Beatle sang a few lines, Michael liked it and the pair began what, for a while, turned out to be a great friendship.

'Off The Wall' sold eight million copies. Michael was the first solo artist to have four top ten singles

from one album. He was firmly established as a musical force to be reckoned with, yet when asked about the album's success he just replied modestly: "It's a start."

Michael Jackson was now 21. Having stamped his authority on his music, it was time to take control of his business life.

First of all he sacked his father. Relations between Joe Jackson and his sons were strained, to say the least. He had ruled the family through fear. His temper was legendary and the fact that the boys were teenage heart-throbs had not stopped him dishing out more than their fair share of beatings.

Michael had never been close to his father and while Joe's intentions for the boys' careers were good, his management style often left a lot to be desired. He was understandably worried about people trying to rip off the family, but his aggressive attitude to business had made him many enemies.

"People are trying to break up the family and I'm trying to hold it together," he said at the time. "The greed for money is what it is. What I'm speaking about is outsiders who see money possibilities."

Joe himself had made some bad financial judgements and the family always seemed to be involved in some sort of legal argument or court case. Michael was fed up with the endless business problems. He wanted to be able to take complete control of that side of his life and delegate responsibility to the best in the business.

The real deterioration in Michael's relationship with his father came when Joe broke the shock news that the brothers had a half-sister they knew nothing about.

Joh Vonnie Jackson had been born in 1974. She was the result of one of Joe's affairs, and he had been looking after mother and daughter financially since her birth.

At one point it looked as if Michael's parents would divorce. They separated on several occasions but every time Katherine went back. Whether or not she was ever able to forgive her husband is unclear, but Michael felt hurt and angry at the pain his mother was going through. He did not even want to be in the same room as his father, let alone have him as a manager.

The man Michael chose to take over his business affairs proved to be another brilliant piece of talent spotting.

John Branca was a smart young attorney with an in-depth understanding of the music industry and an eye for a good deal.

He immediately re-organised Michael's entire financial and business operation. Michael Jackson, already a millionaire, told Branca that he wanted to be the richest and most successful performer in the world.

The lawyer started by re-negotiating Michael's contract with CBS. His royalty rate went up to become one of the highest in the business. The contract was also changed so that Michael could leave The Jacksons whenever he wanted.

The seeds had been sown for Michael's emergence as the world's number one entertainer. His musical ability alone would not have been enough to propel him to the dizzy heights he was about to reach. His amazing business capabilities also set him apart from his rivals.

He had seen the careers of many great artists disintegrate because they surrounded themselves with the wrong people.

Michael Jackson's empire would contain only the best.

Despite the fact that Michael was clearly able to carry off a highly successful solo career without his brothers, he still could not bring himself to break the family ties completely.

Instead of following 'Off The Wall' with a worldwide solo tour, he went back into the studio to start work on the next Jacksons album, 'Triumph'. This led to Michael's first serious involvement in the world of music videos.

The video for 'Can You Feel It' is an amazing journey into Michael's mind. Bathed in angelic light, The Jacksons appear at the creation of the perfect world. They sprinkle sparkling glitter of love across the earth. Children everywhere are caught in The Jacksons' magical spell and look up to the heavens where Michael and his brothers smile down on them.

The theme of a Messiah-like figure sent to spread love and happiness to the world is one that Michael has returned to again and again.

The 'Can You Feel It' film was a breathtaking, pioneering production, years ahead of its time. Michael had decided to turn his hand to videos and in a single sweep had put most of his contemporaries to shame.

The Jacksons embarked on a 36 city tour for 'Triumph'. Michael did not want to go, but his brothers needed the money and once again he went along with the majority.

On stage, Michael was as superb as ever. He incorporated magic into the shows, disappearing in a puff of smoke at the end of 'Don't Stop 'Til You Get Enough'.

Offstage he seemed distant and bored. He found the tour a physical and mental slog. His heart was just not in it.

When the family returned home things got worse. He still mixed with his brothers but when conversation turned to the group, Michael would just change the subject.

He said nothing and they said nothing but everybody knew the truth. Michael Jackson wanted to leave The Jacksons.

All his attention was now focused on his next album. Despite sales of eight million for 'Off The Wall', Michael still felt that he had not been given the recognition he deserved.

His publicists had asked Rolling Stone magazine to do a front page feature on Michael. The editor refused, saying that he did not merit a cover story.

Michael was angry and hurt, but that was nothing compared to his fury at the results of the Grammys. The annual awards ceremony is the American music industry's way of recognising the very best in performing, songwriting and production.

'Off The Wall' was regarded by many as the best album of the year. It had broken records across the world but it received just one nomination, for best rhythm and blues vocal performance.

Michael won, but it meant nothing to him. If anything, he regarded it as an insult. For a performer who took recognition from his peers as seriously as record sales, it was devastating. His sister LaToya was with him when he watched the awards ceremony on television.

"He was very disturbed by it, very depressed. He expected to win much more. He just sat there and cried and cried and cried. Then he got up and said, "My next album is going to be the biggest seller of all time."

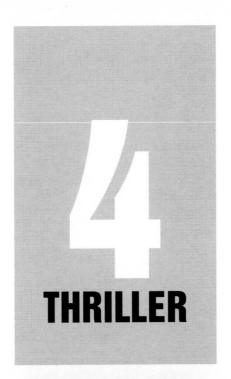

4

THRILLER

It was around 1980 that family, friends and journalists noticed that Michael was behaving rather strangely. He had often appeared shy and somewhat reclusive, and was clearly living in his own little world most of the time, but now his behaviour was becoming distinctly weird.

Firstly, he developed his own unique way of giving interviews.

Michael insisted that his sister LaToya should be present whenever a journalist came to see him. They would all sit in the same room but the journalist was not allowed to speak to Michael. He would direct his questions to LaToya, she would repeat the question to Michael and he would give his answer.

This is an example of this bizarre set up, from an interview Michael gave to London's Capital Radio in 1980:

INTERVIEWER: "I was wondering if Michael ever compares himself to Smokey Robinson as a singer."

LATOYA: "Do you ever compare yourself to Smokey Robinson as a singer."

MICHAEL: "That would be quite nice. Smokey has quite a following, a big audience, but I can't say that I'm as good as Smokey."

It is not clear why Michael chose to do this. It could be that he resented having to give countless interviews but understood that they were necessary to promote his music, and this was his way of making a point. It could simply be that this system gave him more time to think of an answer. The most likely explanation though, is that he was making it clear to journalists that they were dealing with someone different, someone special. Michael Jackson did not live in their world so why should he follow their rules?

Whatever the reason, he carried on giving interviews like this for a year or two, until finally refusing to speak to the press altogether, claiming he was always either misquoted or misunderstood. From this moment, the mystique surrounding Michael Jackson was born. Already an interesting figure, his refusal to explain his actions made him fascinating, and began to generate endless media interest. Michael was well aware of this and he has not given a proper interview since.

Michael Jackson had also become obsessed with his looks.

The spots were beginning to go but he still hated his complexion, his chubbiness, in fact his whole appearance. Michael found the solution partly in his diet. He had become a vegetarian several years earlier, when the idea of eating an animal became just too much.

"Michael is a vegetarian. I mean really a vegetarian," says his father Joe. "He's the type of vegetarian that hardly eats anything. No meat, no fish. He has a cook come in to fix nuts and grapes and things of that sort but that's all."

Michael became fanatical about his diet. He gave up all junk meals, would only eat food that had been organically grown and made sure that he had a constant supply of vitamins.

He had two Sikh cooks to prepare his meals, but often even they would have trouble getting him to eat anything. Michael regarded eating as a chore and more often than not he would simply skip meals.

The result was dramatic. On the cover of 'Off The Wall', Michael, while not being overweight, was by no means thin. But within a couple of years, the chubby cheeks had gone and he had clearly lost pounds in weight.

Magazines would later print old and new photos of Michael Jackson to try to prove that he had had his entire face surgically altered. In truth, he had simply lost weight.

Michael said that his strict diet made him feel fitter and healthier than ever. The press said he was anorexic.

By the early 1980s, close examination of Michael's face led observers to another inescapable conclusion: Michael Jackson had a new nose.

Michael had hated his nose for as long as he could remember. It was wide and podgy, just like his father's.

His brothers called him 'big nose' and it made him feel miserable.

Psychologists have come up with all sorts of elaborate theories about Michael turning to plastic surgery to rid himself of memories of his father and his childhood.

The reality is somewhat simpler. Michael thought that he had a horrible nose, a lot of people in showbusiness had plastic surgery, and if he were going to be the world's number one entertainer, he wanted to look his best. The fact that it meant that he would no longer look like his father was an added bonus.

Michael had been thinking about having a nose job for some time, much to his parents' displeasure. In 1979 an accident on stage made up his mind for him. He fell over and hurt his nose and had to have surgery to fix it.

The operation resulted in a slightly smaller nose, which Michael liked. The surgery left him with some breathing problems, so his plastic surgeon Dr Stephen Hoefflin recommended another operation. Michael used this to alter his nose further. The result delighted him and gave him much more confidence. Whether Michael later went too far with plastic surgery is another matter, but at this stage, it simply made him look better and feel happier.

Family problems continued to cause Michael terrible heartache. In 1980, his eighteen year old brother Randy was almost killed in a car crash. Doctors wanted to amputate his legs but Randy refused and after a long, courageous battle, he made a full recovery.

In 1982 Michael's mother again filed for divorce. His parents were virtually separated for two years before Joe once again persuaded Katherine to give him another chance.

Michael was still living at home and every day he saw the hurt that his mother was going through.

As Katherine's unhappiness increased, Michael's relationship with his father got worse. He loved his mother more than anyone on earth and he could not bear to see what was happening to her. He would sit in his bedroom for hours rather than talk to his father. When they did talk, conversation was strained, especially if it were about business. Joe continued to try to involve himself in his son's career, and was continually coming up with money making ideas that Michael regarded as ridiculous.

However, one of Joe's ideas did go down well with his son. In 1981 he offered to sell Michael half of his stake in the family's home to help him pay off debts.

Michael jumped at the idea. Here was an opportunity to take some control of the family situation and at least guarantee his mother a wonderful home.

He paid Joe an estimated half a million dollars and immediately set about turning Hayvenhurst into his fantasy home.

He re-created Disneyland's Main Street, complete with shops, a soda fountain, and a machine that poured out an endless supply of sweets. There was a swimming pool and jaccuzzi, waterfalls, a 32-seat movie theatre and a video and games room.

He even looked into the possibility of building his own version of his favourite Disneyland ride, Pirates Of The Caribbean, but that proved just a little too expensive and complicated.

Michael made no secret of the fact that he was sealing himself off from the outside world:

"I'm putting all this stuff in here so I will never have to go out there."

Michael successfully turned his hand to producing on the Diana Ross hit 'Muscles'. The song appeared to be about tough, muscular men but 'Muscles' was actually the name of Michael's boa constrictor.

The rest of Michael's attention was focused on just one thing, his next album. Originally it was to be called 'Starlight'. The name was later changed to 'Thriller'.

Along with some of America's top musicians and songwriters, and of course his trusted friend and producer Quincy Jones, Michael went into the studio to start work on what he was determined to make the most successful album of all time.

When people met Michael, he seemed the same shy, reclusive young man. But looks were deceiving. Michael had changed. The failure of the music industry to recognise the success of 'Off The Wall' brought out a tough, aggressive determination that surprised many. For the next few months he worked like a man possessed. Other musicians on the album admit that they found it impossible to keep up with his boundless energy.

On one memorable occasion, one of the musicians asked Michael if he would be disappointed if 'Thriller' sold less than 'Off The Wall'. Michael was furious. He had made it clear that he wanted this record to be the best selling album of all time. It had been his dream since childhood. Now, he finally believed that he was able to accomplish that dream, yet nobody would take him seriously. The musician was told in no uncertain terms that there was no question of the new album selling less than 'Off The Wall'.

Michael and Quincy started with 300 possible songs from which nine or ten had to be selected. It was 1982 and CBS was pushing for the album to be released by Christmas.

"It got to the point where we had four months to finish 'Thriller,'" says Quincy. "As if that wasn't enough, Steven Spielberg entered the picture and talked us into doing the storybook soundtrack album for E.T. I said, 'I can't believe we're doing this right in the middle of Michael's album'. We did two months on E.T. and two months on 'Thriller'. We had two or three studios going at the same time. Van Halen was in one doing the guitar solo for 'Beat It' while Michael was doing vocals next door."

Not surprisingly, Michael had fallen in love with E.T. the moment he saw the film, and he could not refuse Steven Spielberg's offer to record the narrative for the soundtrack album, even though he was supposed to be working on his own new record.

In the studio, Michael found recording the soundtrack a highly emotional experience. When he had to narrate E.T.'s death it all became too much and he broke down in tears.

The making of 'Thriller' was not without its problems. Several weeks after choosing what they thought were their final selection of songs, Michael and Quincy were in the studio listening to one of the tracks. Suddenly Quincy stopped the tape and shook his head.

"What's the matter?" asked Michael.

"It's no good Smelly. There's something missing. If this album's going to be something special we need two more really strong songs."

Rather than be upset, Michael was relieved. The album was sounding good but not good enough. It had to be perfect and thankfully Quincy had realised that too.

Michael disappeared into the studio at home for several days. He emerged with a tape containing two songs. When he played 'Beat It' and 'Billie Jean' his producer just smiled. "You've done it Smelly, this time you've really done it."

In November 1982, Michael, Quincy and several senior CBS executives gathered in the studio to hear the final mix. But when the album finished playing there were no cheers, no hugs or champagne. Instead, Michael ran out of the studio in tears. 'Thriller', his pride and joy sounded, in his own words, "crappy."

The intense pressure from the record company to get it finished had resulted in a rushed job that no one was happy with. The songs were excellent. Michael's singing and the musicians' performances were perfect . . . but the all important mix was totally wrong.

The way an album is mixed is crucial. Getting the balance right between vocals and the music and how each instrument sounds is what makes a special song sound 'special'.

Despite protests from CBS, Michael put his foot down. He told the record company that it was not going to be released until he was totally satisfied with it.

Two days later Quincy and Michael returned to the studio and re-mixed the album, two tracks a week, until it sounded absolutely perfect. When they played it through this time, their reaction was different. It was an amazing album and they knew it.

After 750 thousand dollars and months of hard work and heartache, 'Thriller' was released on 1 December 1982.

The album opened with 'Wanna Be Startin' Something'. A brilliant dance song that had Michael singing about everything from gossips to unwanted babies, it sounded like a natural follow up to 'Don't Stop 'Til You Get Enough' and had actually been written by Michael when he was working on 'Off The Wall'.

The next track, a Rod Temperton song, 'Baby Be Mine' also bore similarities to 'Off The Wall's' 'Rock With You'. That was followed by Michael's duet with Paul McCartney on 'The Girl is Mine'. Michael had wanted to work with Paul ever since he had written 'Girlfriend' for the 'Off The Wall' album. For some reason he phoned Paul on Christmas day and after convincing the former Beatle that it really was him, asked if he fancied recording some songs.

Paul thought about it over his vegetarian turkey and invited Michael over to England. They spent several days in the studio and Michael stayed at Paul McCartney's country estate.

For Michael, working with one of The Beatles was another dream come true. The result of their collaboration was 'The Girl is Mine' and 'Say, Say, Say'.

'The Girl Is Mine' is an unashamedly light and happy pop song which features Michael and Paul playfully fighting over the girl of their dreams. Some critics dismissed it as meaningless drivel, but they were soon silenced when the world heard the next track on the album.

From its eerie opening, to horror actor Vincent Price's spine chilling rap at the end, 'Thriller' is a masterpiece of modern music.

Michael and Quincy Jones-The perfect combination.

Also written by Rod Temperton, Michael knew from the moment he heard it, that this was the song he had been looking for to make his mark. It combined his love of the world of adventure and horror with a superb piece of dance music. Quite simply, nobody had ever recorded a song like 'Thriller'.

Michael Jackson's transformation into a star who was to embrace the whole world of pop, soul and rock was completed on 'Beat It'. Until now, he had been regarded as a soul artist with reasonably wide appeal to the pop market. 'Beat It' smashed down the barriers between soul and rock. Eddie Van Halen's guitar performance made it simply a brilliant record. Michael has always hated his music being classified. To him it is just, music. After 'Beat It', record shops with soul, rock and pop sections had a difficult choice to make in deciding where Michael Jackson's records should go.

'Billie Jean' was nearly called 'Not My Lover' for fear that people would think he was singing about the tennis player Billie-Jean King.

The song is actually about a woman who accuses Michael of being the father of her child. The Jacksons had had their fair share of nutters over the years. People would turn up at their home claiming to be everything from Michael's long lost wife to Jesus.

One woman in particular had been pursuing Michael around the time of 'Billie Jean'. She had sent him several pictures of her and the child she claimed was Michael's. She eventually proposed a suicide pact, and was traced and put in a mental asylum. Despite being surrounded by a tight wall of security, the experience shook Michael. Unfortunately, his song led to the emergence of several Billie Jeans, complete with babies, and

lawyers who wanted a few million from him for child support.

Track seven on 'Thriller' was the beautiful 'Human Nature' written by two members of the group Toto who had had a massive hit with 'Africa'.

'P.Y.T. (Pretty Young Thing)' was written by Quincy Jones and soul singer James Ingram. Backing vocals were supplied by Michael's sisters Janet and LaToya.

The album ended with a love song, 'The Lady In My Life'. During the recording, Quincy Jones remembers his young star being as shy as ever. "On 'The Lady In My Life', I wanted him to sound like he was really begging with a girl. I said, 'Smelly, I want you to beg on this one'. He said, 'No I can't do that'. I said, 'Yes you can'. In the end we closed the curtain in the studio so the engineer couldn't see him and he did it perfectly on the first take."

The release of the 'Thriller' album was not greeted with any great excitement.

'The Girl Is Mine' had come out two months earlier in October, and while it was a hit, it hardly heralded an album that was going to change the world.

Also, the record industry was in a slump. Sales were down everywhere and few expected 'Thriller' to be as successful as 'Off The Wall'.

'Billie Jean', released in January 1983 was an immediate success, reaching number one in Britain and America. But it was not the record or the accompanying video that changed Michael Jackson's life for ever: it was his performance of the song on a TV special to mark Motown's 25th anniversary.

Berry Gordy's idea was to re-create the golden days of Motown, bringing together all the great stars of the era. The highlight of the

show would be The Jackson 5 performing with Jermaine for the first time since the split with Motown in 1975. Four of the brothers thought it was a great idea. Michael refused to take part.

He did not like TV appearances. There was never enough time to rehearse and make sure everything was perfect. Michael was also reluctant to perform with his brothers when his own solo career was taking off.

Michael told his management team to make it quite clear to Motown that he was not going to take part. But his former boss Berry Gordy had other ideas. He knew Michael was the hottest former Motown act around and he was determined to get him to join in the show.

Berry managed to trace Michael to a Los Angeles recording studio. One evening, Michael was inside, editing, when the door opened and in walked Berry Gordy. They greeted each other like old friends, but when the subject of the Motown anniversary performance came up, Michael remained defiant. "Berry, I don't want to do it so don't try to make me change my mind."

But Gordy would not give up. The Motown supremo reminded him of everything he had done for him early in his career, he spoke about the good old days and literally begged Michael to think again and agree to perform with his brothers.

Michael sighed. He was finding it hard to resist Berry's pleas, but if he were going to do him a favour, he wanted something in return.

"O.K. I'll do it. But only if I can sing one of my new songs as well. I want to sing 'Billie Jean' and I want total control over the recording and editing."

Berry Gordy was taken aback. He was not used to artists making

demands of him but he realised that he had no choice. He agreed and they gave each other a big hug.

Michael had made a smart move. He was about to turn what was supposed to be a nostalgic look back to the Motown days of the '60s and early '70s into a celebration of the amazing music of Michael Jackson in the 1980s.

Once he agreed to take part, Michael put his whole heart into the performance. He took charge of rehearsals with his brothers, choreographing a medley of their old Motown hits.

On the night before the performance, he sat in his room at Encino wondering about his own solo part. There were going to be 50 million people watching the Motown anniversary show. Michael knew this was his chance to do something special, but he was not sure what.

He picked up a tape of 'Billie Jean' and wandered downstairs into the kitchen. He put the tape into a machine and as the opening beats started to play, Michael began dancing. He did not stick to a set routine but just let his feet follow the music. Then, during the instrumental break, he tried out the new step he had spent months perfecting. He smiled. Tomorrow was going to be a day he and his fans would never forget . . .

March 25 1983: the star studded audience at the Pasadena Civic Centre in California rose to their feet as The Jacksons took to the stage. The brothers went into a medley of 'I Want You Back', 'The Love You Save' and 'I'll Be There'. Michael and Jermaine put their arms around each other and smiled. All the problems of the last few years were forgotten as the Jackson brothers stood together, united by their one big love . . . music.

When the medley was finished the crowd roared their approval. The other brothers left the stage leaving Michael on his own. "Thank you. I have to say those were the good old days. I love those songs, those were magic moments with all my brothers including Jermaine. I like those songs a lot, but especially I like . . . the new songs."

'Billie Jean' started to play. Those in the audience that night will tell you that what followed was unlike anything they had ever seen or have experienced since.

In the auditorium everybody was spellbound. In front of TV sets, entertainers like Fred Astaire, to many the world's greatest dancer, sat stunned. Michael Jackson's dancing was quite simply, unbelievable. Every move was perfect.

Even without the Moonwalk, Michael's performance that night would have been spectacular, but when he did the magical step, walking forwards and gliding backwards at the same time, there were screams of disbelief from the audience.

The Moonwalk looked impossible. Millions of his fans across the world spent the next few weeks trying to copy it. Few succeeded. Although it became his trademark, Michael did not invent Moonwalking. He had first seen it performed by Jeffrey Daniel of the group Shalamar and invited one of Jeffrey's assistants to his house to teach him the moves.

Ironically, Michael was not completely satisfied with his performance at the Motown anniversary show. After one of the dance spins he had planned to stop, balanced on his toes, for several seconds. He did not stay on his toes for as long as he had wanted and ever the perfectionist, left the stage angry at himself.

The impact his performance had made began to sink in only when an awestruck ten year old boy stopped Michael backstage.
"Hey man. How did you learn to dance like that?"
"Practise I guess." replied Michael.

He smiled. It had taken the approval of a young boy to convince

him that he had done well.

That historic performance was one of the turning points in Michael Jackson's career. Sales of the 'Thriller' album soared. 'Billie Jean' was quickly followed by 'Beat It' and 'Wanna Be Startin' Something'. The release of each single brought Michael millions of new fans. 'Thriller' did not become the world's best selling album overnight. Sales just grew and grew until virtually everyone seemed to have a copy. But that was not just down to the undoubted brilliance of Michael's music. CBS's marketing of 'Thriller' was also superb. Each single plus the accompanying videos was timed precisely to ensure maximum impact. Meanwhile, Michael's image as a mysterious and slightly unreachable star was maintained. He made enough appearances in public to keep interest at a peak, yet when he did appear he said little, just waving at fans with his gloved hand, his eyes hidden behind the ever present sunglasses. Everybody was talking about Michael Jackson and everybody seemed to be buying the album.

Jermaine Jackson says Michael did everything possible to ensure 'Thriller's' success.

"The timing was right. The videos were right. He picked the right people to work with him and the marketing campaign that CBS did was excellent. Everything just fell into place at the right time. There was no way it wasn't going to be the biggest album ever."

The man in charge of marketing 'Thriller' at Epic was Frank Dileo, a shrewd, outgoing, overweight, cigar smoking man who Michael took to immediately.

It was Frank Dileo's idea to release 'Beat It' while 'Billie Jean' was still going up the charts. Many at the record company thought it was too risky, but Dileo understood how massive Michael was about to become. The gamble paid off. Michael Jackson ended up with two records in the top ten at the same time.

Although he was in the process of becoming the world's best selling pop star, Michael did not have a manager at this stage. His father no longer represented him and most of

his business was being handled by his lawyer John Branca. He needed a manager to share responsibility for the increasingly important decisions he was having to make. Someone tough but smart. Frank Dileo was that man. Frank combined the marketing talent Michael needed with an ability to act as a buffer between him and the outside world. Every businessman, promoter and musician seemed to want a piece of Michael Jackson. From now on they would have to get past Frank Dileo first.

As 1983 drew to a close, Dileo's main task was to help Michael top what had undoubtedly been an extraordinary year.

The next few weeks would see the release of the big single, the title track 'Thriller', and Frank Dileo wanted something special to go with it.

The album's videos had already broken new ground, simply by the fact that they were being played on television. Until Michael Jackson, MTV had hardly touched videos by black artists, concentrating instead on white rock performers. The videos

for 'Billie Jean' and 'Beat It' left them with no choice. No TV station on earth, let alone MTV, could ignore Michael Jackson.

For 'Beat It' he wanted to re-create a real life Los Angeles gang scene, so who better to use for the video than real life L.A. street gangs. There were some tense moments when filming started, with extra bodyguards brought in to protect Michael, but the ice was soon broken when he started dancing.

The gang members were genuinely impressed at his talent. In the breaks between filming they would hang out by Michael's trailer where he happily signed autographs and posed for photographs.

The 'Beat It' video featured two warring gangs only too ready to do battle until Michael arrives with his message of peace.

It contained some stunning dance scenes, and although music video was a fairly new concept, it was clear to everyone that Michael Jackson had already become its master. Now, to accompany the 'Thriller' single, he planned the most spectacular music video ever.

The 'Thriller' film is a perfect example of Michael Jackson's determination to always better himself. He had already won universal praise for the album's other videos, and another well produced film with some special dance scenes would have been more than enough to satisfy his ever increasing army of fans. But it was

not enough for Michael. He had decided that the 'Thriller' video was to be unlike anything any pop star had ever produced.

In fact, he did not want it to be like a video at all. Instead, he went about producing what amounted to a short film. To re-create the horror theme of the song, he recruited movie director John Landis, who had made one of Michael's favourite films, 'American Werewolf in London'.

The video ended up as a fourteen minute mini horror epic. Michael is walking home from the cinema with his girlfriend who is still shaking with fear from the werewolf film they have been to see. Under a moonlit sky, they walk past a graveyard where the bodies slowly come to life. Michael and his girlfriend (played by former Playboy pin up Ola Ray) are surrounded by every kind of zombie imaginable. As they close in for the kill, Michael starts to dance. The monsters join in, and he and the ghouls boogie the night away.

It is usual for the record company to pay for a video, but Michael did not want executives breathing over his shoulder telling him that he was spending too much. Money was to be no object, so he informed CBS that he would pay for it. This, in turn, meant that Michael owned all the rights to the film. Yet again, a shrewd move.

The budget for the video was 600 thousand dollars, but they seemed certain to overshoot that even before filming started. Michael's attorney, John Branca, was concerned that he was spending too much, so he came up with the idea for another video on the making of 'Thriller'. This was a fly on the wall documentary on the film's production. It featured the 'Thriller' video in full, together with

Brooke Shields and Michael at the 1984 Grammy awards.

some of Michael's earlier video material and a rare interview with Michael himself.

'Making Michael Jackson's 'Thriller'' went on sale in the shops as a one hour video. Together with a deal with MTV, who paid for the rights to show it first, it meant that Michael effectively got other people to pay for a video that boosted his album sales by several million.

There was one sour note to what was otherwise a highly successful and profitable project. When production had finished and word began to leak out about the 'Thriller' video's contents, the Jehovah's Witnesses made it clear to Michael that they did not approve and would consider expelling him for what they regarded as his dabbling with the occult.

Michael panicked. For several days he went to ground and nobody heard from him. A series of nervous phone calls to John Branca apparently ended with him ordering his lawyer to destroy the entire film. The 'Thriller' video was to be scrapped, and the million dollars it had cost to produce was to

disappear down the drain.

The situation was only saved when John Branca came up with the compromise of putting a disclaimer on the video, stressing that in no way did Michael endorse the occult. He also apologised to the Jehovah's Witnesses. Nevertheless, it proved to be the beginning of the end of the relationship between Michael and his church.

The 'Thriller' single and video and the publicity that accompanied it, increased sales of the album by an estimated 14 million. By early 1984 it had sold a record breaking 25 million copies, making it the best selling album of all time. At a special ceremony in New York, Michael was given official entry into the Guinness Book of Records by publisher Norris McWhirter. It was a freezing cold New York winter's night, but Michael twice went outside to thank the hundreds of fans waiting for a glimpse of their record breaking hero.

The evening was topped for Michael when a telegram arrived from President Reagan:

"Your deep faith in God and adherence to traditional values are an inspiration to all of us. You've gained quite a number of fans along the road since 'I Want You Back' and Nancy and I are among them. Keep up the good work Michael. We're very happy for you. Ronald Reagan."

Three weeks later it was the Grammy awards. Michael had been accepted into the hearts of millions across the world, now he would discover if the industry itself was prepared to recognise his talents, or if he would be shunned, as he had been with 'Off The Wall'.

Michael had two escorts for the night, Brooke Shields, and his twelve year old friend Emmanuel Lewis. Within minutes of the ceremony starting, it was clear that Michael Jackson was going to sweep the board.

He won an amazing eight Grammys; best album: 'Thriller', best record: 'Beat It', best pop vocalist: 'Beat It', best rock vocalist: 'Thriller', best rhythm and blues vocalist: 'Billie Jean', best record producer:

The 'Thriller' video gave the album the final push
needed to guarantee it a place in the record books.
◁

Michael Jackson and Quincy Jones, best children's soundtrack: E.T., best rhythm and blues song: 'Billie Jean'.

Eight times Michael went up to collect his awards wearing his sequinned jacket, rhinestone-encrusted white glove and sunglasses. There were no victory speeches. "This is a great honour. I'm very happy", was one of his longest sentences of the night.

After the ceremony, Michael held a private party in a Los Angeles restaurant, where the guests included Arnold Schwarzeneggar, Bob Dylan and Eddie Murphy. Again, his shyness got the better of him and he left early, but under those shades there was no disguising his delight.

Late that evening Michael sat quietly in the house at Encino. Only the occasional sound from the animals broke the silence of the peaceful Californian night. As he sat there, Michael Jackson looked back at the last few months and felt completely relaxed, totally happy. His whole life had been building up to this moment. He was, without doubt, the most successful pop star in the whole world.

The fans were now ready for the long awaited solo tour which would finally establish Michael as a live performer, away from his brothers. But it was not to be. The rest of The Jacksons were desperate to make the most of Michael's success and tour as a group. Apart from anything else, they needed the money to maintain the extravagant lifestyles to which they were accustomed.

Michael resisted and for a while it looked as though nothing would change his mind. But when his mother pleaded with him to go out on tour one more time to help the brothers, he gave in. He could say

no to his managers, his father and his brothers, but Michael Jackson could never say no to his beloved mother.

Within weeks of agreeing to the tour, disaster struck.

As part of a series of deals to help finance the concerts, The Jacksons signed a sponsorship agreement with Pepsi.

The company had been looking for a new angle in its increasingly ferocious war with its rival Coca Cola. They needed someone who could win over the lucrative youth market. Who better than the pop star who had the best selling album in history? After intensive negotiations between Pepsi and The Jacksons' organisation, a five million dollar sponsorship deal was announced.

Part of the agreement involved Michael making a TV commercial for the company. The ad was to be a mock concert. Thousands of fans were invited to the Shrine Auditorium in Los Angeles to act as the audience. One of the last scenes to be filmed involved Michael walking down a glittering staircase with dramatic explosions just a few feet from his head.

As the cameras rolled and Michael made his way down the stairs to the music of 'Billie Jean', there was a loud bang that shook the stage. When the smoke cleared, Michael could be seen, clearly in pain, grabbing his head. There were screams from the audience as Michael's security men dashed to his side. Jermaine Jackson was just yards from his brother and was convinced that he had been shot, as were many of the crowd. A towel was wrapped around Michael's head and within minutes an ambulance had arrived. It was soon established that a technical problem had caused the explosion. The

medics examined his head and found that he was suffering a second degree burn the size of a palm print on his scalp.

Photographers and TV cameras jostled for space as the stretcher carrying Michael Jackson was eased into the ambulance. His face was covered by the blanket, tearful fans standing nearby feared the worst. Then, just as the ambulance doors were about to close, a hand rose from the stretcher, a hand still wearing the famous white glove.

Despite the pain on the outside, the inside of Michael's head was working fine. When he heard that the press had arrived, he told one of his staff to pass him his glove. The

next morning, pictures of his waving hand appeared on the front page of newspapers across the world.

Diana Ross, Ronald Reagan and Liza Minelli were among the thousands of well wishers who sent cards and flowers to Michael at the Brotman Memorial Hospital. (Doctors had realised that he was not too badly hurt in the ambulance when he said that he had always wanted to ride in a vehicle with sirens.) After a good night's sleep Michael was talking to visitors and watching videos. Then he went on a walkabout, touching patients with

The Los Angeles police department go for a jog
with their latest recruit (far left.)
◁

his gloved hand and signing autographs.

Exactly what had gone wrong during filming of the commercial was not clear, but Pepsi agreed to a 1.5 million dollar donation to set up the Michael Jackson Burns Centre at the hospital where he was treated. After minor surgery, Michael's scalp survived. The Michael Jackson Burns Centre did not. It has since closed because of financial problems.

When Michael was fully recovered, Ronald Reagan invited him to the White House to receive a special Presidential award. Michael wore an elevator operator's jacket given to him the month before by a member of staff at a New York hotel. His acceptance speech during the ceremony on the White House lawn was one of the shortest ever. After a welcoming speech from the President which began with the words, "Well isn't this a Thriller," Michael approached the podium and gave his eleven word reply:

"I am very, very honoured. Thank you very much Mr President."

The 'Victory' tour was a fiasco for Michael from start to finish. The success of 'Thriller' was proof to the most casual observer that Michael Jackson and his management team knew what they were doing when it came to the music business. Yet on important decisions, Michael was constantly outvoted by his brothers.

The family was drawn into a complex web of business deals to try to produce as much money as possible from the tour. Flamboyant boxing promotor Don King took charge of the project, much to Michael's displeasure. King, who would later take over the career of Mike Tyson, launched the tour at a press conference with The Jacksons in New York. The conference started with a fifteen minute

The 'Victory' tour.
Behind the scenes there were many bitter rows.

documentary about . . . Don King. Michael arrived late but when journalists tried to question him, he made it clear that they were wasting their time.

"I really don't have anything to say. I would just like to introduce the rest of my family."

One of the things Michael had tried to tell the family was that ticket arrangements for the tour were a rip off. Firstly, they were thirty dollars each. Michael wanted them to be twenty. The family voted on it and he lost. But as the 'Victory' tour's keyboard player Rory Kaplin remembers, that was not the only problem.

"They were only allowing four tickets to a family, so when we got down to the bible belt of America where people have six or seven kids, they were really angry because they had to choose between their children, to decide which ones could go to see The Jacksons.

The fiasco over the tickets led to a fierce backlash in the press, and when Michael started receiving letters from fans accusing him of exploiting them, he decided enough was enough. He called a family meeting and told his brothers that they either had to change the arrangements or they could count him out of the tour.

Two days before the first concert, Michael held a press conference and announced that the distribution of tickets was changing and that all his profits would be going to charity.

The 'Victory' tour kicked off in Kansas City in July 1984. Tension between Michael and his brothers was high. They were on separate floors in hotels. Michael had his own jet, the others used normal airlines. The Jacksons were offered several million dollars for the video rights of the tour, the other brothers thought it was a great idea, Michael

refused and once again threatened not to perform unless they backed him. Any pretence of The Jacksons being a democratic group were gone. They would vote, and if Michael was outvoted, he would simply threaten to quit. Frustrated but powerless, his brothers had no choice but to let him have his way.

Despite the backstage bickering, Michael was determined not to let the fans down when it came to the actual concerts. They were spectacular; lasers, explosions, some superb magic, and of course the music. The highlights of the shows were the medley of the old Jackson 5 hits and the songs Michael performed from 'Thriller.'

Once each concert had finished, it was not all arguments and animosity. They were, after all, brothers and managed to find time to go back to the old pranks; buckets of ice cold water over the doors, throwing Frank Dileo in the swimming pool and throwing water filled balloons at unsuspecting hotel guests below.

For the press, the tour's highpoint was when Bruce Springsteen dropped in at Michael's hotel for a chat. The conversation between Wacko Jacko and The Boss went like this:

MICHAEL: "I hear your concerts are really long?"

BRUCE: "Yeah, I play for about three hours."

MICHAEL: "Wow, how do you manage it?"

BRUCE: "I take a half hour break in the middle. I just love playing that's all."

MICHAEL: "And is it right you tell little stories during the concerts?"

BRUCE: "Yeah, I tell stories. People like to hear your voice."

MICHAEL: "Oh I couldn't do that. I'd feel people were learning

something about me they shouldn't know."

BRUCE: "I stay up until about four after a concert, what do you do?"

MICHAEL: "I watch TV or read. I can't go to sleep."

BRUCE: "Don't you ever go out?"

MICHAEL: "I can't. Too many people would bother me."

And that was it. The two great giants of rock. They were both with the same record company but apart from that they could have come from different planets.

The Jacksons played more than 50 concerts in five months during the 'Victory' tour. The 'Victory' album also produced the collaboration with Mick Jagger on 'State of Shock', which was released as a single.

Michael's brothers wanted the tour to go on to Europe, but he had had enough. The others had all made around seven million dollars from the concerts. It was time to say goodbye.

On 9 December 1984, The Jacksons played the last concert of the tour in Los Angeles. The rest of the family knew that Michael was fed up but they never really believed he would leave the group permanently. His farewell at the end of the concert left them in little doubt:

"This is our last and final show. It's been a long twenty years and we love you all."

Michael Jackson had left The Jacksons.

5

WHO'S BAD?

As The Jacksons finished the 'Victory' tour at the end of 1984, the world's attention was focused on a crisis of devastating proportions in Africa.

When Michael returned home and saw the TV pictures of the children dying in the Ethiopian famine, he broke down in tears. Millions faced starvation and the world seemed powerless to stop it.

In England, Bob Geldof of the Boomtown Rats had seen the same pictures and decided to stir the rock world into action.

The result was the Band Aid single 'Feed The World' which topped the charts in dozens of countries.

In the USA, music manager Ken Kragen took control of the American music industry's anthem for the starving, which was to be called 'We Are The World'. Ken wanted all the big names to appear on the record, but would the elusive Michael Jackson agree to take part?

"The original thought in getting Michael involved in USA For Africa was as a performer," says Ken, "but when I got Quincy Jones to call him, he not only said yes to performing, he also said he wanted to help write the song."

It was decided that Michael should get together with Lionel Richie and that they should both write the music and lyrics. Ken Kragen says they made a great team.

"Lionel Richie wrote the 'We Are The World' part of the chorus and gave a tape of that to Michael, who then went into the recording studio on his own and wrote the rest of the music. Michael and Lionel then got together and finished the lyrics. Michael says the words just poured out of them. He's always been convinced the song came direct from God."

On Monday January 28, 1985, the biggest collection of rock stars ever to gather in one studio, arrived in Los Angeles: Bruce Springsteen, Paul Simon, Diana Ross, Stevie Wonder, Smokey Robinson, Tina Turner, Billy Joel, Bob Dylan, Bob Geldof and many more.

When they arrived, Michael was already laying down tracks for the chorus. As the evening progressed, he was his usual quiet, shy self, spending most of the time with his friends Diana Ross and Stevie Wonder, and helping Quincy Jones with the production. At 8 o'clock the following morning, it was finished.

'We Are The World' went on to raise millions for the starving. Later, Michael was asked for a statement on the situation in Ethiopia:

"When I was asked to write the song, I put my soul into it. I put my heart into it. That...was my statement."

During the 'Victory' tour, Michael had done a sitting for a sculptor flown out to America by the famous Madame Tussaud's waxworks in London.

In March 1985 he went to Britain to unveil his waxwork. Most of Michael's schedules are kept secret to try to keep the crowds at

bay. This visit was not. The 'Victory' tour had not gone to Britain and thousands of fans packed the roads around Madame Tussaud's in the heart of London, hoping for their first ever glimpse of Michael. Traffic was brought to a standstill and police lined the streets to try to contain the screaming fans.

Inside, Michael posed for photographs alongside his waxwork dummy, and was so delighted he even broke one of his own rules by speaking to the press and telling them, "It's wonderful." Outside, the chaos turned to pandemonium when Michael emerged, and to the alarm of his security men, leapt on top of his limousine to wave to the crowd. Minutes later, he was in the car and gone...leaving his adoring fans sobbing and hysterical, but happy.

Back in California, Michael had a cheque for 60 million dollars waiting for him, his royalties from Epic for the sales of 'Thriller'.

Life now presented Michael Jackson with a big problem. If producing 'Thriller' had been his greatest ever challenge, that was nothing to the task of a follow up album that had to be even more successful.

But before work on the new album could start, Michael had to complete a film that he was making for Disney. The company had approached him and asked if he was interested in collaborating for a new Disneyland ride. Michael, a huge Walt Disney fan, was only too happy to oblige but instead of just helping to invent a ride, he wanted to create a whole new Disney experience. The result was 'Captain EO', a seventeen minute 3D film that was only to be shown at Disneyland in California, the Epcot centre in Florida and later at EuroDisney in France. Set in a

special theatre with a tilting floor and smoke that pours from the screen, 'Captain EO' is a short but spectacular sci-fi epic directed by Francis Ford Coppola. Michael plays the space travelling hero who fights to save a planet by doing battle with its evil Queen. The film features two songs: 'Another Part Of Me' and the unreleased 'We Are Here To Change The World'.

Michael describes the film as a celebration of good over evil. It was certainly a celebration of money and time.

'Captain EO' cost 20 million dollars and took over a year to make. The star actor's bizarre behaviour during filming caused more than its fair share of problems. For a start he would not work on Mondays. Michael hates Mondays, so he does what most people dream of doing at the beginning of the week... he stays at home.

He also refused to take off his sunglasses on the set of 'Captain EO', except when he was certain that filming had started. On top of that, Michael insisted on the music being as loud as possible, so loud that the film crew had to wear earplugs.

Rehearsals would stop when Michael's friends turned up to say 'hello'. One memorable occasion was a food fight with Elizabeth Taylor, another was when Michael

disappeared for a whole afternoon and was discovered hiding on one of the other sets. He thought it was hilarious. The producers, whose bills were rising rapidly, were less sure.

Michael was well looked after during filming. Every day he turned up with his entourage of bodyguards, cooks and make-up artists. A big hit with the fans, 'Captain EO' was a double triumph for Michael; it gave him the lead role in a highly innovative movie, and a permanent place in the Walt Disney history books.

Those honoured enough to get a glimpse of Michael Jackson's bathroom in 1985 and 1986 saw a big sticker on the mirror with '100 MILLION' written on it. That was how many copies of his next album he was determined to sell, more than double the sales of 'Thriller'. Anybody who tried to tell Michael that he was being unrealistic was met with a cold stare. The next couple of years were clearly going to be tough going.

Work on 'Bad' started in 1985 when Michael played around with a few songs in the studio at his house.

When he makes records, Michael does everything through singing. Surprisingly, he is not an accomplished musician. He sings the sound he wants, then passes the tape to his guitarists and keyboard players who turn it into top class music.

By the following August, Michael and Quincy Jones were ready to choose between the 62 possible songs they had selected. They spent another year in the studio and at times, both became very frustrated. Everyone knew that Michael was a perfectionist, but the target he had set himself of making an album more popular than 'Thriller' seemed to be making him push himself too hard.

He was never satisfied, recording tracks over and over again, although Greg Phillinganes who played keyboards on the album says his determination was understandable.

"He didn't change into an ugly monster or anything but with Michael, every project has got to rise above the previous one. He's very committed and a very strong visionary. He knows exactly what he wants."

While the recording of 'Bad' was tense at times, Michael says working with Quincy Jones made all the hard work worthwhile. "What I love about working with Quincy is that he's unlimited musically. Whatever you want, he can do: jazz, folk, pop, classical, soul, gospel... anything. It was just wonderful working with him."

Quincy and Michael became great friends, more like father and son than producer and musician, although Quincy still found him terribly nervous. "He really is shy and if he wants to sing a song for me he makes me sit on the other side of the couch. I have to close my eyes and turn out the lights and then he'll sing the song. Ninety thousand people are no problem but me, his producer, that's different."

By early 1987, pressure was growing to finish the album fast, especially with a world tour just months away. But Michael delayed for as long as he could. It was as if he were scared of unleashing the album on the public, terrified of failure.

He should have had more faith in himself. 'Bad' was released in September 1987 and immediately hit the number one spot in eight countries.

It did not get great reviews, and the album's title gave the critics a field day, but there was no stopping the fans. Millions bought it in the first few months and they loved it.

The first beats of the opening track, 'Bad' showed Michael in heavier, funkier form than on 'Thriller'. The song tells the story of a boy who returns to his tough neighbourhood after being away at private school. In his book 'Moonwalk', Michael tells us the song means, "that when you're strong and good, you're bad." Michael had offered Prince the chance to sing with him on the track. Prince refused.

The accompanying video was shot on the streets of New York by top director Martin Scorsese. It cost 2 million dollars. Again, there were reports of tension on the set with Michael insisting on take after take, until he was completely satisfied.

Track two on 'Bad' was 'The Way You Make Me Feel', an uptempo love song with a good dose of 'Aows' and 'Acha-oohs'.

'Speed Demon' was to crop up later on the 'Moonwalker' film in a scene that featured Michael

Man in the mirror:
Michael with his waxwork at Madame Tussaud's.

The 'Bad' tour broke records worldwide.
Over fourteen months Michael played to 4.5 million
people.

Sharing the limelight with guitarist Jennifer Batton,
whose image was transformed by Michael for
the tour.
▷

speeding along on a motorbike wearing a rabbit mask!

'Liberian Girl' is a beautiful love song that produced an equally wonderful star studded video in which Michael plays a movie director filming all his friends waiting for him to turn up for his own video shoot.

'Just Good Friends' was Michael's duet with Stevie Wonder, written by the same team responsible for Tina Turner's 'What's Love Got To Do With It'. (Michael wrote nine of 'Bad's eleven songs.)

'Another Part Of Me' was already known to those who had seen 'Captain EO' and eventually became the album's sixth single.

For the fans, the special song on the album was 'Man In The Mirror'. To those who just hear Michael's music on the radio, he is simply the provider of great pop songs. For his devoted fans, the songs mean a lot more. 'Man In The Mirror' was Michael's personal message to them, that you have to change the way you live before you can change the world. For many, it is the best Michael Jackson song ever made.

Michael says that he had no one special in mind when he wrote 'I Just Can't Stop Loving You', but was thinking of someone when he recorded it. It was the first single from 'Bad' and reached number one in July 1987.

'Dirty Diana' became the fifth number one from the album, and 'Smooth Criminal' produced a spectacular gangster video, although Michael had to argue with Quincy Jones to persuade him that the song was worth featuring on the album.

'Leave Me Alone' (which only appears on the 'Bad' CD) was written as a love song, but its message was clear. It was aimed at the press, who seemed determined

to hound Michael for the rest of his life. The video showed Michael being pursued by journalists, in the form of dogs, as he journeyed through a mysterious world containing, among other things: a shrine to Elizabeth Taylor, a dancing skeleton and newspapers with the headlines: 'MICHAEL CONFIDES IN CHIMP' and 'MICHAEL WEDS ALIEN'.

All in all, 'Bad' tried to portray a tougher, if still slightly strange Michael Jackson. The cover showed him in a leather studded suit, after another shot of his face behind a veil of black floral lace was rejected by the record company as being too 'soft'.

'Bad' produced five number ones; 'I Just Can't Stop Loving You', 'Bad', 'The Way You Make Me Feel', 'Man In The Mirror' and 'Dirty Diana'.

The tour that followed broke records wherever it went. Sponsored by Pepsi to the tune of 15 million dollars, it was one of the biggest rock tours the world had ever seen. During 123 concerts, Michael played to a total of 4.5 million people. It was not enough for him to just go out and perform. He insisted that every concert should be a complete showbusiness experience.

With the help of the latest technology, he was able to re-create his videos on stage, complete with breathtaking special effects and magic. Michael would disappear from one side of the stage and re-appear seconds later at the other side, in a completely different costume.

The 'Bad' tour kicked off in Japan in September 1987, complete with 137 staff, eight truckloads of equipment including 700 lights, 85 costumes and two huge video screens.

Michael played to one million people in Europe alone. In London he broke the record for seven sell out shows at Wembley Stadium. At one of the London concerts, he presented Prince Charles and Princess Diana with the night's profits which were to go towards children's charities. Michael was thrilled at meeting the royals and even offered to give Prince Charles dancing lessons!

At another of the Wembley shows, Michael stopped the concert after twenty minutes, and in a tearful voice asked his surprised audience to say a prayer for Elizabeth Taylor.

"A very dear and close friend of mine, Elizabeth Taylor, is very sick right now. I would like everyone to bow their heads for five seconds as a mark of respect."

Michael dedicated 'I Just Can't Stop Loving You' to her, and cried again later during 'She's Out of My Life'.

Liz Taylor was, indeed, very ill in America. But the prayers seemed to work and she soon made a full recovery.

Michael had recruited some of the best musicians in the world for the tour. Guitarist Jennifer Batton walked into rehearsals sporting mousy brown hair and a pair of glasses. Michael took one look and told her to dye her hair white and get some contact lenses. As a result, Jennifer spent much of the tour at the front of the stage with Michael. "He wanted me to stand out and it was his idea to dye my hair. It shows how clever he is because when you see the pictures of the concerts, I really stick out."

There was a set routine for the whole tour: three days of concerts, then four days off. Michael kept himself to himself and because the entourage was staying in different

Michael's fans were more than a match for the British police when he arrived in London.

Michael thanks the officers who helped to protect him during his visit.

Michael with Princess Diana after a concert at London's Wembley Stadium.

Michael Jackson tour merchandise is a multi-million dollar business.

Pepsi's 15 million dollar sponsorship of the 'Bad' tour was rock's biggest ever commercial endorsement.

hotels, the musicians would often go for several weeks only seeing Michael on stage.

"We didn't have a lot of contact with him," says guitarist Jennifer Batton. "He was always out of the stadium before the end of the shows for security reasons. But some of the days we did spend with him and it was just a ball. We went to the Tokyo Disneyland. Michael had the whole place shut down. We'd go on the rollercoaster, then when we were done they'd ask if we wanted to go again instead of waiting in line. We did that in two or three cities."

Keyboard player Rory Kaplin says he was always amazed at how committed the fans were during the 'Bad' tour.

"It was like Beatlemania. He's got some real hardcore fans. They'd camp out in hotel lobbies for five days before we got there, just hoping to get a glimpse of Michael. In Europe we'd do these huge stadium dates and in places like London the fans would get there at 1 o'clock in the afternoon, which meant they were out in the sun for seven or eight hours before the show started. It was hot and sweaty, people were passing out and having to be dragged from the crowd. That was kind of gruesome."

Jennifer Batton says there was massive security, twenty four hours a day. "Michael seemed pretty calm and relaxed for the whole tour but I don't know how he coped. Sometimes we'd be in the same hotel and it was impossible to move because of the hundreds of kids trying to get a glimpse of him. He had eight security guards with him all the time, and whenever he wanted to go anywhere it had to be planned in advance. Security would be alerted, Michael would leave through secret exits and if he wanted to go shopping the store would have to be closed down for him. I can also say that

Michael totally pampered us on the tour. We had the best hotels and lived in complete luxury. He's a sweetheart."

Drummer Ricky Lawson says Michael made sure that he got all the musicians together just before the shows started to say a prayer.

"We just asked God to watch over us and make sure everything went O.K... that nobody got hurt and that the audience felt the spirit of the show, and that we all do this for the glory of God and that everybody can have a good time. Michael is very religious. He might not go to church every Sunday but a lot of it is just what he feels inside."

The tour had many highlights. Michael played a concert in Leeds in England on his 30th birthday where 90 thousand fans sang 'Happy Birthday'. On the last leg of the tour in America, he went back to the Motown studio in Detroit where his career had started and handed over a cheque for 125 thousand dollars to help set up a Motown museum. "I'm happy and proud to give back to the soil from which I came," he told his old Motown boss Berry Gordy.

For Michael and the musicians it was an exhausting but wonderful tour. Their shows had been some of the most spectacular that pop fans had ever seen. In Los Angeles in January 1989, Elizabeth Taylor, Berry Gordy, Diana Ross and Princess Stephanie of Monaco joined the tens of thousands of fans who stood, cheering and clapping at the end of the last concert of the tour.

Nobody could say that it had not been a tremendous success. Michael though, was still not completely satisfied. He was happy with the tour, but deeply disappointed that the 'Bad' album had only sold 20 million copies. It was still a long way ahead of any other performer, but it did not compare with 'Thriller's' 40 million,

and against the target of 100 million that he had set himself, it was a distinct failure. He made it clear to his staff that he was not happy, even though friends like keyboard player Greg Phillinganes tried to tell him that he was over reacting. "I said to him that sales aren't everything. It's about how good the music is. Because 'Bad' sold less than 'Thriller', it doesn't make it any less of an album. I think the music is at least as good as 'Thriller.'"

The 'Bad' tour had certainly taken Michael to new levels as a performer. Yet his manager Frank Dileo announced to distraught fans that this was the last time Michael Jackson would ever go out on the road.

"Michael is retiring from touring," said big Frank. "There's no way he'll be able to top these concerts and he's just had enough."

The fans who knew Michael best were not so sure.

6
WHO'S MAD?

Those who have met Michael Jackson think of him as a kind, caring, shy and reclusive person. The world's press portray him as a mad Peter Pan figure, obsessed with toys, animals and children and with a face falling apart from plastic surgery. The truth is a complex but somewhat less dramatic combination of the two.

Michael's 'weirdness' goes back to his childhood. When the world tries to make judgements about him, it compares him to normal people. Michael Jackson has never lived a normal life. At the age of six he was touring clubs and colleges and performing up to twenty concerts a week. At the age of ten he was one of the world's most successful pop stars. He spent his teens closeted from the outside world, and by his early twenties he was unable to venture out without being mobbed by adoring fans. It is hardly surprising therefore, that he has tried to re-live the childhood he never had. It is also not surprising that, away from the harsh realities of normal life, he indulges in what seem to be rather strange fantasies.

The 'Wacko Jacko' label began to stick in the early 1980s. By the time of 'Thriller', it was clear that

Michael had had plastic surgery on his nose. Some journalists were convinced that he had let his surgeon loose on his whole face, altering his lips and eyes and trying to whiten his skin.

Speculation was also rife about his love life, or rather lack of it. For a pop star this successful not to have a string of women in tow was almost unheard of. Michael Jackson seemed more interested in his diet and pets than sex!

At first, Michael liked the extensive media attention that his curious lifestyle generated. But by the 'Victory' tour in 1984, the rumours and lies were upsetting him deeply and he was worried that

his fans were starting to believe the stories.

In September 1984, Michael's manager, Frank Dileo, took the unprecedented step of calling a news conference to publicly deny the allegations being made. He read out this statement from Michael Jackson:

"For some time now, I have been searching my conscience as to whether or not I should publicly react to the many falsehoods that have been spread about me. I have decided to make this statement based on the injustice of these allegations and the far-reaching trauma those who feel close to me are suffering.

I feel very fortunate to have been blessed with recognition for my efforts. This recognition also brings with it a responsibility to one's admirers throughout the world. Performers should always serve as role models who set an example for young people. It saddens me that many may actually believe the present flurry of false accusations.

To this end and I do mean END –

No! I've never taken hormones to maintain my high voice.

No! I've never had my cheekbones altered in any way.

No! I've never had cosmetic surgery on my eyes.

Yes! One day in the future I plan to get married and have a family.

Any statements to the contrary are simply untrue. Henceforth, as new fantasies are printed, I have advised my attorneys of my willingness to institute legal action and subsequently prosecute all guilty to the fullest extent of the law.

As noted earlier, I love children. We all know that kids are very impressionable and therefore susceptible to such stories. I'm certain that some have already been

Michael has had between four and six operations on his nose. This is not as excessive as it appears. Plastic surgeons have one golden rule when advising people on how far they should go in having their appearance altered. If it makes them feel better about themselves and does not involve any great risk, then it is O.K. For people in showbusiness, a trip to the plastic surgeon can be almost as common as a visit to the dentist. Given Michael's intense dislike of his chubby nose and the fact that he is able to use the best doctors available, it is hardly surprising that

The changing faces of Michael Jackson. Over the years his carefully chiselled nose has thinned through plastic surgery. But are the other changes natural or man made?

hurt by this terrible slander. In addition to their admiration, I would like to continue to keep their respect."

It is Michael's plastic surgery that has generated most interest. If all the stories were true, Michael would have no face left at all. It has been said that he has had nine or ten nose jobs as well as alterations to his cheeks, lips, eyelids and skin pigmentation.

Michael's plastic surgeon is sworn to secrecy and only he and Michael know the real truth, but it has been possible to establish some of the facts. It is thought that

he decided to opt for surgery. As for reports that he has had ten operations on his nose, that is extremely unlikely. After five or six, there would be very little left to work on.

Michael has also admitted having a small dimple put in his chin. Quite why, nobody knows.

He insists that this is the limit of the surgery but few seem to believe him. Experts claim that he has also had cheek implants and his lower lip thinned. Journalist Mike Walker of America's National Enquirer newspaper has been following Michael's activities for more than ten years:

"I don't know whether his face is melting but I do know the medical profession feels he has gone overboard. Prominent plastic surgeons I've spoken to feel it's almost unhealthy to have the amount of surgery he's supposed to have had. The doctors don't like the idea of a person coming back again and again for more. On the other hand, Michael is an entertainer so you could put it down to him wanting to look better and better."

This claim of excessive plastic surgery is contradicted by Juliette Simkins of Madame Tussaud's waxworks in London. She regularly

sees Michael and has to assess whether he has changed enough to merit a new waxwork.

"That so called famous plastic surgery has been very exaggerated and we know because we've seen him over the years and studied him. We did two waxworks of him in the 1980s but you must remember that people do change. We made Prime Minister Margaret Thatcher four times in ten years."

The press have delighted in showing old and new pictures of Michael, comparing them and coming to the conclusion that he has had his face totally re-shaped. Plastic surgery has certainly played

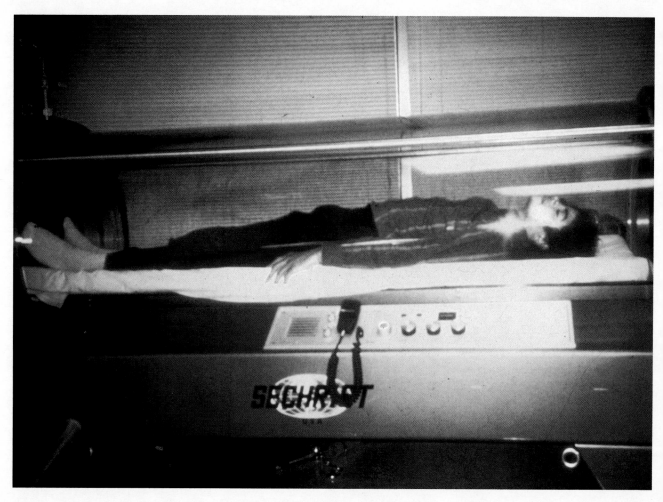

its part, but so have the natural changes that everybody undergoes. One of the main differences is the chubbiness which has gone completely from his face. This is due to his strict vegetarian diet. Michael eats nuts, dried fruit, steamed vegetables and little else. In fact his cooks have trouble getting him to eat regularly at all. Michael does not particularly like food. On Sundays he fasts and has nothing except a couple of glasses of orange juice. It is therefore understandable that his face often looks gaunt, and has changed considerably over the years.

The other widespread belief is that Michael has had complicated treatment on his skin to make him look whiter. He has consistently denied this and there is no proof that he is not telling the truth.

What people seem to be overlooking are the effects of good make-up and lighting. When Michael re-emerged in 1991 after a three year break, everybody claimed that his skin was visibly lighter on the video for 'Black Or White'. It did look lighter... but so did his chest and arms when he ripped his shirt off. Is it really credible to suggest that Michael has had the colour of the skin on his entire body changed because he hates being black?

Michael has had plastic surgery, possibly quite extensive surgery, but he regards the details as strictly personal. It is sufficient to say that most of what is printed about that surgery is a gross exaggeration.

Michael is fascinated by medicine. He has studied dozens of medical books and is also reported to have stood in on operations to get a first hand experience of the intricacies of surgery.

After having his wisdom teeth removed, his dentist gave him a surgical mask to protect him from germs. Most patients only have to wear the mask for a couple of hours. Michael spent most of the next few weeks with his mask permanently in position to keep him germ free!

When Michael was in hospital after burning his head during the Pepsi commercial, he was shown a hyperbaric oxygen chamber. The chamber is a glass casket which feeds extra oxygen to burns victims to help their wounds recover.

Michael was very curious. His doctors, who were getting used to his new found interest in anything medical, happily answered all his questions. One doctor apparently told Michael that he had a theory that sleeping in the chamber could help you live longer...There are two versions of the events that followed in the amazing story of Michael and

The famous hyberbaric oxygen chamber. The press were told that it was part of Michael's plan to live to 150.
◁

the oxygen chamber.

The first is that Michael became obsessed with the idea that the chamber could help him live longer. He wanted to live to 150 and here was the answer. He tried out the chamber, and a photograph of him sleeping in it was leaked to the press. Despite warnings from doctors that excessive use of the chamber could be dangerous, Michael offered thousands of dollars to the manufacturers to supply him with one. They refused.

This story made headline news across the world. Wacko Jacko had finally flipped.

There is, however, another theory about the story; Michael was shown the chamber in hospital, heard about claims that it could make you live longer and realised that this was an opportunity for some great publicity. He arranged

for his management to leak a story saying that he was using the chamber to make him live longer. The accompanying photograph was given to an American magazine by a third party who assured them that it was genuine.

Although everyone involved has kept tight lipped about the incident, it seems that the second is the most likely explanation. Michael had realised that his reputation for being weird was something he could take great advantage of.

Another story that convinced everyone that Michael was crazy, came when it was revealed that he wanted to buy the remains of the Elephant Man from a medical museum in London.

The story of John Merrick, who lived in the 19th century and whose hideous deformities had earned him the nickname 'The Elephant Man',

had been turned into a film starring John Hurt. Michael cried every time he saw it. He read several books about the case, and when he heard that the Elephant Man's remains were kept at the London Hospital Medical College, he reportedly offered one million dollars to buy them.

The accuracy of this story has again been thrown into doubt. Although Michael's publicists issued a press release confirming that he wanted to buy the skeleton, the medical college claimed to know nothing of such an offer. They also made it clear that they were not interested in selling.

If the story was planted by Michael to generate more publicity for his forthcoming 'Bad' tour, it served its purpose. But it also opened the floodgates to dozens more totally untrue stories about him. By the time the 'Bad' tour started, the 'Wacko Jacko' publicity campaign, designed to show what a strange, mysterious person Michael was, had backfired. The world was convinced that Michael Jackson was completely mad.

Mike Walker of the National Enquirer newspaper has been responsible for many of the stories on Michael.

"The best way I can pin it down is to say that he's very good at getting publicity and some of these things are definitely calculated, but he is also a very weird lad. We call him 'His Imperial Weirdness.'"

By the late 1980s, a catalogue of stories had been printed about Michael's strange behaviour. He talked to his chimpanzee Bubbles, he had wallpaper with Elizabeth Taylor's picture on it, he had a shrine to Liz Taylor in his house and had even asked her to marry him. He wanted Princess Diana in his next video, his nose was about to

Michael Jackson's fairground. Just part of Neverland Valley's 2,700 acres.

fall apart and he was furious at Prince for using his psychic powers to drive Bubbles the chimp mad.

Bubbles was the centre of much of the press attention. Michael was often seen in public with him and even took him on tour.

They were clearly great pals, but their friendship led to the inevitable questions about why Michael seemed to get on better with chimpanzees than he did with human beings.

LaToya Jackson remembers the day Bubbles arrived at the family home in Encino.

"At one point, Michael, our mother and myself wanted to adopt a child. Everyone else had left home and we wanted to bring another child into the house. We ended up getting Bubbles instead and just treated him like another member of the family."

It was Mike Walker of the National Enquirer who ran the most controversial story about Bubbles.

"There was a great furore when I reported exclusively that Bubbles the chimp had died, been stuffed and was being kept inside Michael's home. I double checked the story before I ran it and I had it confirmed from some very good sources. Michael's people immediately called a press conference and denied it, although they never made an official complaint to me or my paper. So I said, 'Fine, if Bubbles is alive, bring him forward, and when you do, we will have an expert on hand to compare the new Bubbles with pictures of the old Bubbles. Then even though one chimp looks much like the other we'll be able to tell whether that was the true Bubbles, or at least the Bubbles that was supposedly Bubbles back when Michael was carrying Bubbles around!"

The offer was turned down.

Michael has never made a secret of his love of animals.

"I'm crazy for them," he told writer Steve DeMorest. "Birds, puppies, I love them all, especially exotic things. I've had llamas, peacocks, a rhea which is the second largest bird in the world, a macaw which is the largest parrot from South America, pheasants, racoons... everything."

Michael even admitted talking to his llamas. "I have a wonderful relationship with them, they really understand me. I make this crazy vocabulary and they understand and come running."

Michael's ever increasing collection of animals was one of the reasons that he decided it was time to move away from the family home. There was simply not enough room for the llamas, fawns, rams, giraffes, snakes, parrots, monkeys, swans, peacocks and horses.

He also wanted some independence away from the constant family pressures to perform again with his brothers.

After months of searching, he found his paradise home on the outskirts of a small town called Los Olivos in the California Valleys, an hour and a half's drive from Los Angeles.

Sycamore Ranch was a twelve bedroom mansion set in a massive 2700 acre estate. Built in the style of a Danish farmhouse, it had wonderful sprawling rooms and amazing gardens, complete with its own lake and fifty thousand oak trees.

When Michael heard that it was up for sale, he toured the ranch in a horse drawn carriage and fell in love with it immediately.

It was beautiful, and large and secure enough to let him lead his own life, completely sealed off from the outside world.

He bought Sycamore Ranch for 17 million dollars and immediately turned it into his dream home, renaming it 'Neverland Valley' after his love of Peter Pan.

As you drive into the quaint town of Los Olivos, there is no obvious sign that the home of the world's most famous pop star is just up the road. The main street has no more than a dozen stores, catering for the town's population of 150 and the constant trickle of tourists.

About a mile away, as the country road starts climbing up the mountains, there is a gate, with a security guard in a wooden hut on the other side. Nothing of the wonders inside are evident from the front gate, and a buzz on the intercom produces emphatic denials from the guard that this is the home of Michael Jackson. The privileged few who have been allowed through the gate know better.

For the first few hundred yards the road continues, surrounded only by green fields. Then a sign warns to beware of children playing. On either side of the road are bronze statues, and a short drive later, Neverland Valley comes into view. The house is huge, and matched only by the breathtaking sight of the grounds, with lakes and

bridges surrounded by flower gardens, all playing beautiful classical music.

Michael's pride and joy is his zoo. Children can play with the llamas or sit on the giraffes, other visitors can take the horses out for a ride through the fields and woods.

A few months after Michael moved in, there was a fire in the giraffe house. The giraffes were rescued but they came within minutes of death. Michael did not want it happening again. He set up the Neverland Fire Brigade and spends several hundred thousand dollars every year ensuring that fire engines and crew are constantly on site.

The house also has its own cinema, showing all the latest movies for Michael and his guests. Then there is the arcade house, with dozens of arcade machines (all free) as well as a juke box, pool tables and an ice cream machine that makes frozen custard.

Up in the hills of Neverland is the museum house, packed with Michael's memorabilia collected from a lifetime in showbusiness; stage gear, sequinned gloves and the famous jacket he wore at the 1984 Grammy awards.

The house itself has a games room full of toys, and a library and music room complete with a wonderful grand piano. Guests stay in their own suites which come with a lounge area and bathroom.

Music manager Ken Kragen is one of the few people Michael has taken around his private rooms.

"His house is like a personal Disneyland with all kinds of exotic animals. He has every sort of games machine you could imagine. There's also a funny old movie car you can drive around the house. Michael showed me his bedroom which is really unusual. He's got a loft which is his own little hiding place where he goes to read. His bedroom is really strange because it's full of

mannequin dolls like you see in shop windows. They're like real people, all with their own different style of clothes."

Journalist Mike Walker claims to have discovered some other fascinating facts about Michael's home.

"One of the first things he did after moving in was have a huge tank built and filled with his favourite mineral water. He actually got them to put in a system that lets him bathe and have his toilets flushed in this expensive water. When I first got this story, I thought no, this is too much, it must be Michael trying to get some publicity. So we checked with the water company and it turned out to be absolutely true. He had this huge tank built and the trucks from the mineral water company pull up to the ranch and fill it up."

Mike Walker says Michael's obsession with health even extends to his toilets.

"There are these new toilets from Japan which are unique, because apart from fulfilling all the usual functions, they analyse your blood pressure and check your heart. They cost seven thousand dollars each and Michael has had his whole house fitted out with them."

There are no other houses around Neverland. Opposite the front entrance is a small school that Michael occasionally visits.

His nearest neighbour is George Moore.

"This is pretty much the middle of nowhere but I think that was the idea. He wanted to have a big area away from the city. He usually leaves in a helicopter, other times we see him go in and out in a limo. The security's very tight. They always have guards at the gate and they do regular checks along the

outside fence to make sure people aren't trying to get in. We have fans up here but it's impossible to get in if you're not invited."

George often sees Michael with groups of underprivileged children brought over from Los Angeles. "He has them there for the day, shows them his zoo animals and takes them on his amusement park rides."

There is no doubt that Michael is as fond of children as he is of animals. His friendship with boys like actor Macauley Culkin who he even took on holiday to Bermuda, have raised a few eyebrows, but as Michael himself has explained, when it comes to choosing between children and adults, children win him over every time. "They are one of the main reasons I do what I do. Children know everything that people are trying to find out.

So many people think certain things are childlike, but grown ups are really nothing but children who have lost all that real magic by not noticing and digging and finding out. I believe in that deeply."

On tour Michael spends as much time as possible with children. His musicians hardly ever see him but drummer Ricky Lawson thinks that is quite understandable.

"He loves kids because they're honest. When they say something it's straight from the heart and really children are the only group of people Michael can trust. They're not friends with him just because he's Michael Jackson. They genuinely love him. He's spent time with my children and they always have a wonderful time."

One of Michael's favourite pastimes is going out in disguise with his young friends. He will often go down to the slum areas of Los Angeles dressed as a drop-out, although the ever present bodyguards sometimes give the game away.

The fancy dress trips can go badly wrong. On one occasion Michael went into an antiques shop in Atlanta dressed as a tramp. The owner started making racist remarks at which point Michael hid in a wardrobe. When he finally came out, Michael went to put his hand in his pocket. The shop owner claimed that he thought he was going for a knife. He hit Michael and knocked him to the floor. The police were called and found a clearly terrified tramp, who after several minutes managed to persuade them that he really was Michael Jackson.

Another favourite haunt of Michael's, both in and out of disguise, is Disneyland. Occasionally he will go there late at night when the rides are closed to the public, but more often than not, he will be sneaked in, and wearing the famous sunglasses, whisked to the front of the rides. By the time people recognise the famous face sharing a ride with them, he is rushed away to another part of Disneyland through the maze of secret corridors that run underneath the magical kingdom.

If the stories circulating about Michael during the 'Bad' tour helped encourage the image of a totally bizarre human being, he did nothing to contradict that image with the release of the 'Moonwalker' film. The one and a half hour movie was a combination of archive material on Michael's career, footage from the 'Bad' tour, the 'Leave Me Alone' and 'Smooth Criminal' videos, and the film's centrepiece: another struggle between good and evil with Michael saving the universe through his musical and magical powers. The special effects and dance sequences were superb, although the film as a whole was a curious mix. It cost

Michael a staggering 27 million dollars to make. Distribution problems meant that it was never shown in cinemas worldwide as he had wanted, although it did bring in millions in video sales.

Throughout the success of the 'Thriller' and 'Bad' years, Michael kept his strict adherence to the Jehovah's Witnesses religion. He attended services every week, even on tour. Sister LaToya says he also stuck to the Witnesses famous tradition of knocking on people's doors to try to persuade them to join the faith.

"Even on the 'Bad' tour he would try to go door to door in disguise as often as he could. He would perform at night, then the next day, whatever town he was in, he would go from door to door."

LaToya had also been a strict follower of the faith, and as a teenager had spent hours every week studying the bible with her brother. In the end though, she turned out to be the reason Michael left the religion.

When LaToya decided to leave the Jehovah's Witnesses, the church told Michael that he must never speak to her again. His faith had already been stretched to the limit by the church elders' harsh criticism of his music and dance routines, but this was the final straw. He wrote to the church leaders explaining that his love of God had not changed, but that he no longer felt able to follow the Jehovah's Witnesses faith.

Since leaving the Witnesses, Michael has kept his religious beliefs very much to himself, although those close to him say that he is still very devout, often prays and has a deep belief in God.

Ironically, Michael did stop speaking to LaToya shortly after this incident, although it had nothing to do with religion.

Since their childhood, Michael and LaToya had been inseparable. She had stayed at Encino with him when all the other brothers and sisters had left. When Michael was making 'Thriller' and 'Bad' she was probably his closest friend, and the new songs were always tried out on her.

The problem for LaToya was that she had never shared in the rest of the family's success. She had released some records, but none had been particularly successful and despite subtle hints from the family that perhaps her talents lay elsewhere, she insisted on pursuing a career as a performer.

Things began to go badly wrong for the family when LaToya teamed up with manager Jack Gordon. Her parents claimed that he kept her prisoner. LaToya said that was rubbish and claimed in turn that her parents had tried to kidnap her. Whatever the truth, Michael and his family went for several months hearing nothing from her. The bombshell came when LaToya announced that she was going to pose naked in Playboy. Michael phoned her and begged her to change her mind, but she refused, and the pictures appeared with LaToya wearing nothing but a snake wrapped around her body.

Michael reportedly severed all contact with LaToya after the Playboy photos were published. Her parents were devastated, but worse was to come. LaToya married her manager Jack Gordon, although she admitted they were not in love, saying that it was purely a marriage of convenience to keep her family at bay. Gordon then disclosed that his new wife was writing an

Sister LaToya with mother Katherine.

The two Michaels – Jackson and Crawford, at a performance of 'The Phantom Of The Opera'.

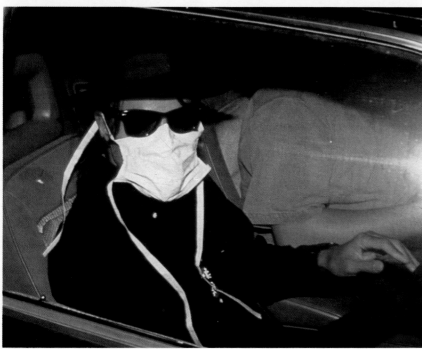

Janet Jackson admits there is a 'friendly rivalry' between her and Michael.

Elizabeth Taylor is one of Michael's closest friends.

autobiography that would 'blow the lid' on life in the Jackson family.

The book was published in 1991. In a series of interviews in which she came close to tears, LaToya spoke of how she and other members of the family had been abused as children by their father Joe. The rest of the family claimed the allegations were a pack of lies.

The book resulted in a public slanging match between LaToya and her parents, with Joe and Katherine begging her to come back to the family. Their words seemed to have some effect. In 1992 LaToya announced that she was divorcing her husband/manager Jack Gordon. She accepted an offer of a residency at the famous Moulin Rouge nightclub in Paris and relations with the family seemed to show a slight improvement.

Throughout the controversy, Michael kept his distance, refusing, publicly at least to take sides. He was clearly furious at his sister, although interestingly, in her book and the accompanying interviews, LaToya hardly ever had a bad word to say about him.

For the rest of the family, life was offering mixed blessings. Janet was going from strength to strength. Her 'Rhythm Nation' album produced a string of hits, a highly successful tour and established her firmly as an artist in her own right. In 1991, she signed a 32 million dollar deal with Virgin Records. Until Michael signed an even better contract a few weeks later, it was the most lucrative record deal ever.

Things were not going so well for the Jackson brothers. They had recorded an album without Michael; '2300 Jackson Street'. It had poor sales and their record contract was not renewed. For a family used to living extravagantly, this was a problem. Michael made it clear to his brothers that they would have to fend for themselves. He had had enough of supporting them.

This brought inevitable accusations of Michael being selfish with his money. Surely someone who was reported to be worth 300 million dollars could spare some cash to look after his brothers?

There were stories that Marlon faced homelessness because Michael would not pay his mortgage. But it was not the money that bothered Michael, it was the constant pressure from one or other member of the family wanting either financial assistance, or to share in Michael's success, namely by re-forming The Jacksons. He had, after all, earned them each 7 million dollars by reluctantly agreeing to join the 'Victory' tour.
If they could not look after their money, that was their problem, not his.

The bad feeling that had been simmering in the family burst out for the world to see when Jermaine Jackson released a song, clearly directed at his superstar brother.

'Word To The Badd' had lyrics that included: "You changed your shade, was your colour wrong? Think they love you, they don't know you. Lonely superstar."

Jermaine was unrepentant about recording the song. He claimed that Michael had refused to take his phone calls and this was the only way of communicating with him.

"I tried to call him and tell him how I was feeling but I couldn't get through to him. So I wrote the song and I wrote it from my heart. It's a message from an older brother to a younger brother, an attempt to bring him back to the family and an attempt to heal our relationship. People might say I'm jealous but I love the fact that he's as big as he

is. The song is about having him come back to reality because he's not in touch with reality at all. I can say that because I'm his brother."

If it were not jealousy, it sounded a lot like it. It is easy to feel sympathy for the brothers who have seen Michael's fame and fortune grow while theirs has declined, but until they accept the situation and stop attacking Michael for his decision to go it alone, they will only succeed in making themselves feel more bitter and pushing him further away.

Those who observe Michael Jackson will put forward all sorts of theories about his plastic surgery, his fascination with childlike things and his diet. But there is one area of his life that nobody seems to have successfully unravelled. Journalist Mike Walker:

"The biggest mystery about Michael Jackson which no journalist has solved is, what is Michael's love life like? There are all sorts of rumours. One is that he developed a distaste for sex when he was on tour with The Jackson 5. His brothers used to bring girls up to the room right in front of him, even though he was a little boy. There are a thousand rumours and the truth is, nobody knows. I'm convinced he's kept his love life secret from everyone. Even the people closest to him don't really know what goes on."

Michael is often seen with escorts at important occasions. They have ranged from Tatum O'Neal to Brooke Shields, Elizabeth Taylor and even Madonna. But the last proper 'girlfriend' was Tatum O'Neal back in the 1970s, and there is considerable doubt even about that relationship.

Michael faces a terrible problem in trying to form meaningful new

friendships. Everybody he meets seems to love him, but most love him simply because he is such a big star. Other pop stars can turn to the people they knew before they were famous. Michael has been famous for as long as he can remember.

Michael has said that he would like to get married and have children. He has even suggested that if he did, he would give up performing.

For those who want to try to work out the secrets of his love life, there are two simple options. Either Michael has some deep dark secrets, or he is telling the truth and is just waiting for Mrs Right to Moonwalk into his life.

A rare insight into Michael's character came from his autobiography, 'Moonwalk'. It is without doubt a highly selective account of his life, but in it, Michael also describes some of the family tensions, notably between him and his father. He tells of the pressures of fame, his loneliness, and the hurt he feels at much of the public criticism he suffers. 'Moonwalk' leaves many questions unanswered, but it does succeed in painting a picture of a caring, sensitive, and determined, if slightly eccentric person.

There is little doubt that Michael finds the constant barrage of attacks on him, mainly from the press, very upsetting. When the stream of bad publicity reached its peak on the 'Bad' tour, Michael broke his vow of silence and agreed to answer one question from People magazine journalist Todd Gold. Todd asked him what misconceptions the public had of him. Michael gave this written reply:

"Like the old Indian proverb says, do not judge a man until you have walked two moons in his moccasins. Most people don't know me, that is why they write such things in which most is not true. I cry very, very often because it hurts and I worry about the children. All my children all over the world. I live for them. If a man could say nothing against a character but what he can prove, his story could not be written. Animals strike not from malice, but because they want to live, it is the same with those who criticise, they desire our blood, not our pain. But still I must achieve. I must seek truth in all things. I must endure for the power I was sent forth, for the world, for the children. But have mercy, for I've been bleeding a long time now.

M.J."

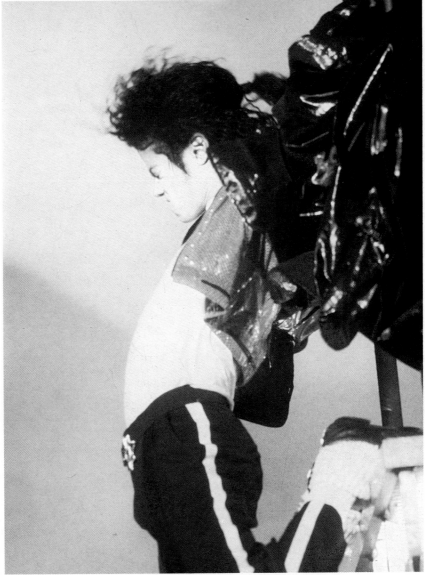

7
DANGEROUS

Michael began the 1990s with a formidable list of achievements behind him. Over the last ten years he had sold an amazing 110 million records. He had made the best selling album of all time, 'Thriller' and the two top selling albums of the decade, 'Thriller' and 'Bad'. He had also had one of the most successful rock tours ever. But things were not all sweetness and light in the Jackson camp.

Firstly, Michael was not happy with the 20 million sales of 'Bad'. However unrealistic his target of 100 million, that was the goal he had set himself, and he and those around him had failed to achieve it.

He was also angry at the confusion that had surrounded the 'Moonwalker' film. Although video sales re-couped his costs, he had wanted the film to be shown in cinemas worldwide. It was released in Japan and parts of Europe, but in America it was only available on video. Someone was to blame and it certainly was not Michael.

It is not clear which, if any of these problems was the reason for Michael sacking his manager, Frank Dileo, but sack him he did. Michael's ruthlessness in business affairs is a little known fact which

shows there is more to Michael Jackson than meets the eye. He is shy, and often appears nervous and embarrassed in the company of others, but underneath the quiet exterior is a tough businessman who does not tolerate fools gladly. Throughout his quarter of a century in the music business, he has made a careful study of how the industry works. This, combined with his ability to recruit the best managers, lawyers and financial experts available, has made the Jackson empire and his company MJJ Productions a force to be reckoned with.

Michael had shown his shrewd business sense back in 1984 when

he bought the publishing rights to the Beatles songs for 47.5 million dollars. The purchase was the end of Michael's friendship with Paul McCartney, although it had been Paul who had first drawn Michael's attention to the financial benefits of investing in publishing. While they were recording 'Say Say Say,' Paul told Michael that he owned the rights to dozens of songs and every time they were used, he earned money. Their conversation ended with Michael saying, "Maybe I'll buy your songs one day."

He had been joking, but at his next meeting with his attorney, John Branca, Michael asked him to find out if there were any good songs for sale. It turned out that there were: the entire Beatles catalogue, owned by ATV music.

In the 1960s, the Beatles had signed away their publishing rights. Paul McCartney had tried to buy them back but the asking price was always too high. It was not too high for Michael Jackson. He could not think of a better way of confirming his status in the music world than owning the songs of the most successful group ever.

When Paul McCartney heard of Michael's acquisition, he was

furious. As far as he was concerned they were his songs and nobody had the right to try to take them away from him. Michael was unrepentant. To him it was a straight business deal. Paul McCartney had had his chance to buy and let it pass.

As a result of the purchase, everytime a Beatles record is bought, played on the radio or used in a commercial, Michael Jackson makes money.

The incident was proof to anyone who needed it that Michael could be tough when it came to business. Manager Frank Dileo knew this better than most, but his sacking still came as a bolt from the blue. Michael's attorney John Branca, who had skillfully steered him through the success of 'Thriller' and 'Bad', was equally surprised. He was even more surprised when, a few months later, a letter arrived on his desk informing him that his services were also no longer required.

Michael's new manager was Sandy Gallin, who already handled The Pointer Sisters, Whoopi Goldberg and Dolly Parton. Another influential name in Michael's business affairs was David Geffen, whose highly successful Geffen Records had artists including Cher and Guns 'n' Roses. One of the richest men in the American music industry, Geffen guided Michael through many of the important business decisions surrounding his forthcoming album and tour.

The original idea for the follow up to 'Bad' was a double album called 'Decade', which was to contain several of the hits from the 1980s, along with a handful of new songs. 'Decade' should have been released by the end of 1989 but Michael was uneasy about the project. As he worked on the songs he realised that he was easily capable of producing enough material for a completely new album. Plans for 'Decade' were scrapped and Michael began work on what was to become 'Dangerous'.

Before he became fully engrossed in the album, Michael had a few visits to make and awards to collect. He went to see children at the Cleveland Elementary School in America where five students had been killed by a gunman. He also went to the White House for a reception with President Bush, received the Entertainer Of The Decade award, won a Grammy for the 'Leave Me Alone' video and was named the world's highest paid entertainer for the second year running.

The whirlwind stopped abruptly on 3 June 1990. Michael was in the middle of a strenuous dance session at Neverland Valley when he felt a sharp pain in his lungs. He clutched his chest, gasping for breath. The room was spinning but Michael managed to get to a phone to call his personal physician (and plastic surgeon) Dr Stephen Hoefflin, who dashed to the house and rushed an increasingly panicking Michael Jackson to hospital, shaking and sweating. He was sedated to calm him down and doctors carried out a series of tests. In the end, it just turned out to be an anxiety attack apparently brought on by business worries. Doctors again warned Michael to take things easy.

He stayed in hospital for several days and was delighted to discover that his room was just down the corridor from Elizabeth Taylor, who was herself recovering from one of her serious illnesses. Michael spent hours at her bedside and, according to Miss Taylor, he played a crucial part in her recovery.

When he left hospital, Michael set about devoting his entire energies to the 'Dangerous' album. Once again, he set himself a target. 'Dangerous' had to top 'Thriller' as the world's best selling album and this time there were to be no mistakes.

Michael realised that for him to reach his goal, the album would have to be very, very special. The world was tumbling into an economic recession. People had very little money to spend and record sales, like everything else had suffered. This was not the best time to be planning a 50 million selling album.

On top of that, Michael was astute enough to realise that he had other serious problems. Although

he had been out of the public eye since 'Bad', his name had never been out of the headlines for long, usually linked to totally ludicrous and untrue stories. He was regarded as a joke by many, who doubted whether his music in the 1990s would be able to win over as many fans as it had in the last decade.

Not only did the music on the new album have to be the best, Michael's image also needed an overhaul. He accepted that he would always be regarded as a strange figure, but the wilder stories about him just had to stop. Michael made it clear to his staff that he wanted no more ridiculous stories leaked to the press. If anything, he wanted a 'harder' image put over to the public.

He also wanted a tougher edge to his music. Rap and dance was as popular as ever, Michael believed

that if he could turn his hand to some heavier dance tracks and combine them with a collection of superb pop songs, he would hit just the right note with 'Dangerous'.

Firstly, he decided not to use Quincy Jones on the album. Quincy had produced 'Off The Wall', 'Thriller' and 'Bad', and his contribution to Michael's success can never be over exaggerated. But Michael knew exactly what he wanted and believed that he was now capable of overseeing most of the production himself, although he brought in top producer Teddy Riley on some of the dance tracks.

Quincy Jones was quite happy to leave the project to Michael. He was running his own musical empire and simply did not have the time to devote to a new Michael Jackson album. The pair remained firm friends. In 1991 Michael actually agreed to do an interview for a documentary film about Quincy, although the questions were sent to him in advance and when he recorded the interview he insisted on all the lights being turned off. The result was a sequence in 'Listen Up, The Lives Of Quincy Jones', where Michael's voice was heard but the screen was black.

'Dangerous' ended up taking three years to make and cost more than 10 million dollars. This time, Michael's determination to make the album perfect exceeded anything that had gone before. He would often work eighteen hours a day and he and his musicians would spend weeks just working on one track. If Michael was not 100 per cent satisfied, the whole song would be scrapped. Keyboard player Greg Phillinganes was one of the musicians who had to keep up with Michael's punishing schedule.

"I played on 'Dangerous' and I know everyone talks about how long it took to make, but I think that speaks for itself. It's a very strong album and I think the fans agree, just look at the charts. With 'Dangerous' Michael just wanted to better himself again. He's never prepared to rest on his laurels. It's that Jackson thing. It's all about getting better."

Greg says Michael is always great fun to work with, even though he clearly felt under a great deal of pressure during the album's recording.

"Michael's very easy going in the studio. Obviously he's the boss but it's not as if he walks around with a tag on his head saying, 'I'm in charge'. We also have a very structured way of doing things. We start by recording the drum part, then we'll go to a string part, then we'll record the bass and the main guitars and then Mickey goes in to record the vocals. It's like making a big sandwich. You start with the bread and you make sure all the necessary ingredients are mixed appropriately."

The album should have been released in early 1991, but Michael kept postponing it, still not happy with the finished product. "I'm never satisfied with anything. After I've cut a track I'll come home and say, 'Oh no that's not right, we've got to do it again' and we just go back and back and back and finally you say, 'Darn it, I should have done this, I should have done that' and it's number one in the charts and you're still screaming about what you should have done. I think it's good just to keep growing and perfecting and I'd like to stay that way, because if you're satisfied with everything, you're just going to stay at one level and the world's going to move ahead."

As the weeks and months passed, Michael's record company grew increasingly nervous. CBS had been taken over by the Japanese firm Sony. In March 1991, Sony announced that it had signed a new six album contract with Michael said to be worth up to one billion dollars. It included plans for albums and films which would come under the umbrella of the new Jackson Entertainment Complex.

According to some reports, the deal, which made Michael the highest paid pop star ever, included a 3 million dollar gift from his record company, a 15 million dollar advance and a royalty rate of 25 per cent, compared to an industry norm of around 12 per cent.

At the news conference to announce the deal, it was confirmed that 'Dangerous' was set for release in June.

June came and went, still with no sign of the album. However, keen Jackson watchers could see that the carefully orchestrated publicity campaign leading up to the release was underway.

First of all, Michael appeared in public with Madonna. They went to the Oscars together and later dined in a plush Los Angeles restaurant. (Michael's cook was sent to the restaurant in advance to prepare a special vegetarian meal.) There was talk of Madonna appearing on one of the album tracks, or of the pair recording their own single. Nothing came of either suggestion although Madonna said that she had used her meetings with Michael to try to persuade him to change his dress sense and come up with a 'tougher' look.

Michael's voice also made an appearance on an episode of 'The Simpsons.' He portrayed a fat white man called Michael Jackson who was sharing a room in a mental

Michael hosted Elizabeth Taylor's wedding and gave the bride away.

hospital with Bart's dad Homer. The man told Homer that he had committed himself to the hospital in 1979 because his 'Off The Wall' album had only got, "one lousy Grammy nomination."

If the timing of Elizabeth Taylor's wedding to Larry Fortensky at Michael's 'Neverland Valley' home was a coincidence, then it was a remarkable one. It was, without doubt, the closest that America has ever been to a royal wedding, and it took place less than a month before the release of 'Dangerous.'

When Liz Taylor told Michael that she was getting married, he immediately asked if he could host the wedding. The two had always been very close. As both had been childhood stars they felt that they had a lot in common, and for Michael this was an ideal way of paying back years of friendship.

Michael took on responsibility for everything and paid for the whole event, even giving the bride away. Elizabeth Taylor was amazed at how much effort he put in.

"As soon as I told Michael about the wedding he insisted on taking charge. What I didn't count on was how lavish his plans would be. I asked him about the costs but he just brushed it aside saying that one of the greatest joys in his life is giving pleasure to other people."

Michael spent over 100 thousand dollars on flowers alone and ordered ten thousand candles for the ceremony. He even arranged for a string quartet to play to the newlyweds when they retired to Neverland's 'Royal Suite.'

On the day of the wedding, the world's attention was focused on the little town of Los Olivos and the home of its famous resident. The press had been banned from the wedding, but undeterred they took to the skies in planes, hot air balloons and even hang gliders to try to get shots of the wedding party. The pictures of Michael that did appear were the first to show his new look for 'Dangerous', with his hair longer than anyone could remember.

The master tape of 'Black or White' was flown into Britain on Concorde, strapped to two burly security guards. The situation was the same worldwide. Never had there been so much secrecy surrounding one record.

For the first time ever, Sony had set up an elaborate synchronised worldwide radio release of the single. Copies of 'Black or White' were delivered to major radio stations in all the main capital cities at exactly the same time and sent to others on a special satellite link.

'Black or White' was a tantalising taste of what was to come on the new album. It was a pulsating mixture of rock, dance and rap, with a special appearance by Slash of Guns 'n' Roses on guitar.

The song hit just the right balance between the Michael Jackson everybody knew and the exciting new sound that he was about to unleash on the world.

With a staggering 200 thousand pre-sale orders in Britain alone, the single was guaranteed the number one position.

It was as if Michael had never been away. He was back on the cover of virtually all the music magazines and again dominating the headlines in the press.

The publicity that was to follow in the weeks and months ahead had been carefully planned a long time in advance, not least the furore that surrounded the video for 'Black or White.'

Michael was determined that his re-emergence would make a massive impact. He hired John Landis who had directed the 'Thriller' video, to make the most expensive and exciting musical film the world had ever seen.

The result was an amazing eleven minute video for 'Black or White' which cost an estimated five million dollars to make. The film starred Macauley Culkin and Norm from 'Cheers'. It opened with Norm (the grumpy father) being blasted into space when Macauley (the disobedient son) starts playing his electric guitar. Using the very latest production and editing techniques, the video also featured Michael dancing in locations ranging from Russia to the Wild West. The last five minutes contained no music but showed Michael in a violent dance routine that included him smashing up a car.

It was certainly spectacular but in the eyes of many TV bosses it was also excessively violent. When the video was shown simultaneously to 500 million TV viewers in 27 countries, most stations showed the film with Michael's destruction of the car cut out. In England the BBC refused to show it saying that it was "gratuitous violence, not suitable for family viewing."

Two days later a spokesman for Michael Jackson said that the offending section had been removed from the video and would not be shown again. It seemed like a climbdown but Michael was delighted. Everything had gone as planned and the launch of the first single from the album had been a total success: number one across the world and backed by a video that everybody was talking about and that portrayed the rougher and nastier side of Michael Jackson.

The stage was set for 'Dangerous'.

Amid unprecedented security, the master tape of 'Black or White' was flown from America to Britain handcuffed to two security guards.

November 1991. Fans started queuing at record shops early in the morning to make sure that they were front of the queue for the first copies of the new album.

Its fourteen tracks spanned 76 minutes and the entire breadth of modern music, from dance to funk, rap, rock, ballads and gospel.

The album opened with the searing dance beat of 'Jam'. Any doubts that Michael would not be at the forefront of nineties music were quickly dispelled. With the help of producer Teddy Riley, the computer pop of 'Bad' had been replaced by funky guitar and synth style R&B hip hop. Riley produced all of the album's heavier dance songs. He had made his name as America's pioneer of so called 'New Jack Swing' dance music. Little had been heard of his work outside the U.S.A.

but a few months in the studio with Michael Jackson soon changed that.

Track two, 'Why You Wanna Trip On Me' had much the same message as 'Leave Me Alone', namely why, with massive problems like famine, AIDS, homelessness and drug addiction, did the world want to 'trip' on Michael Jackson?

'In The Closet', the album's third single was the track that Michael had apparently asked Madonna to sing on. The credits for the duet on the album sleeve just said, 'Michael Jackson and mystery girl.'

'She Drives Me Wild' could have been the follow up to 'Speed Demon' from 'Bad', although like most of 'Dangerous', it had a much heavier dance feel.

'Remember The Time' produced the album's second single and a wonderful video in which Michael

gets to kiss glamorous model and actress Iman and perform in front of a king, who on closer inspection turns out to be Eddie Murphy.

'Can't Let Her Get Away' completed the first, dance orientated section of the album and opened the way to a total change of mood with 'Heal The World.'

A few months after the release of U.S.A. For Africa's 'We Are The World', Michael had heard a version of the song recorded by children. That stuck in his memory and for 'Heal The World', he incorporated children into the song, their voices blending beautifully with his own.

The album version of 'Black or White' included a re-enactment of the video, with a young Michael Jackson fan battling it out with his father over whether or not he should turn his music down.

In clubs, the bass on songs such as 'Who Is It' sent shivers down the spine. The album had been superbly mixed to ensure the maximum impact, whether it was heard on hi-fis, radios or in clubs.

On 'Give In To Me' Michael showed once again that he could move from dance to rock with ultimate ease. Michael's new friend Slash did the honours once more on guitar.

'Dangerous' is full of surprises and 'Will You Be There' was one of them. Michael took a risk by spreading his musical net so far, but his talent and immense experience shone through on this unashamedly joyous and uplifting gospel track. He sang it on MTV's tenth anniversary show surrounded by choirs of children. At the end of the performance, an angel descended and embraced Michael. It left many in the audience in tears.

Michael's close friend and co-producer Bruce Swedien remembers the recording of 'Keep The Faith' only too well:

"When he came to put the lead vocal on, Michael sang the first and second verses and then disappeared," Bruce told Rolling Stone magazine. "It was very unlike Michael and when I went to look for him I found him standing in the corner of his office crying his eyes out. We had tried it in two keys and unfortunately he had picked the wrong one. He was absolutely heartbroken. I told him to pull himself together and said we weren't going home until we'd finished. We didn't leave the studio until dawn."

'Gone Too Soon' was Michael's personal tribute to Aids victim Ryan White. Ryan had fought a courageous battle against the authorities who had tried to stop him going to school because of the

disease. Michael and Ryan became great friends and Ryan had been to stay at Neverland Valley before his death. Michael was devastated when he died. He went to the funeral and continues to support charities set up in Ryan's name.

Michael saved the title track until last. For 'Dangerous', it was back to the pulsating dance beat that was to become the album's trademark.

The cover of 'Dangerous' was almost as varied and fascinating as the music inside. Michael wanted to move away from the traditional photoshot cover. The finished artwork, which took six months to create, is an intricate array of images which loosely follow the theme of a circus attraction. The familiar Michael Jackson eyes stare out, with his animal friends dotted around for good measure. They include: an antelope, elephant, bison, hare, swan, fish, tortoise, wild boar, peacock, baboon, butterfly, chaffinch, walrus, wasp, rhino, gazelle, frog, and of course Bubbles.

The man in the bow tie is circus king TT Barnum. There is a very young Michael Jackson, a skeleton, presumably the Elephant Man, a young boy with an 'M' on his shirt who's thought to be Macauley Culkin, another boy holding another skeleton, and an eye which is the Greek symbol of good luck. The image in the middle of the picture symbolises the toil of the world.

There is one other particularly interesting item on the sleeve notes of 'Dangerous'. There had been much discussion, encouraged by LaToya's book, about relations between Michael and his father. They had certainly been strained, but whatever his faults, Joe loved his children dearly and was very upset at suggestions that he had mistreated them. Michael made his

position clear by dedicating the album to: "My dearest parents, Katherine and Joseph Jackson".

In the early days of its release, the press caught on to the idea that 'Dangerous' was a flop. "Jacko Floppo" was one headline.

They could not have been further from the truth.

'Black or White' had topped the charts in more than twenty countries, matching the success of 'Billie Jean' and 'Thriller'. In America it became Michael's tenth million selling solo single, staying at number one for seven weeks.

'Dangerous' sold a staggering two million copies in America alone in it's first six weeks of release. In Britain it sold one million. In Australia, 310 thousand copies were bought in the first month, making it the country's fastest ever seller.

By February 1992, just four months after it's release, 10 million people across the world owned a copy of 'Dangerous'.

In 1992, Michael broke eight years of silence and finally agreed to do an interview to explain the album. He told Ebony magazine that he regarded himself as a messenger from God, sent to earth to share his gift of divine music and dance. He also believed that in the future, 'Dangerous' would be regarded as one of the greatest pieces of music of all time.

"I wanted to do an album that was like Tchaikovsky's 'Nutcracker Suite', so that in thousands of years from now, people will still be listening to it. I would like to see children and teenagers and parents and races all over the world, hundreds and hundreds of years from now, still pulling out songs from that album and dissecting it. Something that will live forever."

8

HEAL THE WORLD

"The only reason I am going on tour is to raise funds for the newly formed, 'Heal The World Foundation', an international children's charity that I am spearheading to assist children and the ecology.

My goal is to gross 100 million dollars by Christmas 1993. I urge every corporation and individual who cares about this planet and the future of the children to help raise money for the 'Heal The World' charity.

The foundation will contribute funds to paediatric AIDS in honour of my friend Ryan White. It will also offer support to such worthwhile organisations as Children's Diabetes, Minority AIDS Foundation and other charities.

I am looking forward to this tour because it will allow me to devote time to visiting children all around the world, as well as spreading the message of global love in the hope that others too will be moved to do their share to help heal the world.

Thank you for coming. I love you all very much."

*MICHAEL JACKSON FEBRUARY 1992-
RADIO CITY MUSIC HALL NEW YORK.
NEWS CONFERENCE TO ANNOUNCE THE
'DANGEROUS' WORLD TOUR.*

Few had believed Michael in 1988 when he announced that he would never tour again. Live performance was in his blood. The thrill of getting up on stage to entertain was not something he could give up.

His promise to himself to make 'Dangerous' a best seller also meant that a tour was necessary to make sure the whole world knew about his new album.

But the overriding force that sent him back on the road was his deep desire to do something really special for the world's children.

Michael believes that he has a God-given duty to help children. He sees the success he has achieved as a further sign that he must use all his talents to help those less fortunate than himself. His devotion to sick and dying youngsters has always been a very private matter. With a few exceptions, he has insisted that this is the one area of his life that is kept well away from the glare of media attention.

When he is on tour, sick children are brought to his room night after night. Many are close to death and have to be wheeled in on hospital beds. Those who work with Michael often find the visits too upsetting and leave the room, but he will reach out to the children, take their hands and speak quietly to them.

Michael also visits hospitals, and once he gets to know a child, he will keep in touch, often phoning them to check on their progress.

"I tell the kids, 'I'll see you next year,' and sometimes the thought that I'll be back next year makes them hang on. That's happened several times. People told me this girl was about to die, but I kept running into her three years in a row. The fourth year she died but the doctors couldn't do anything and for me to come in and help give her the gift of life really makes me feel good."

If they are well enough to travel to his ranch, Michael will invite youngsters to Neverland Valley and spend hours playing with them in his games room and on the fairground rides. Michael's friendship with AIDS victim Ryan White left him determined to work even harder for children. By organising a world tour around his very own charity, Michael realised that he would be able to spread the message that more needed to be done for the young, while raising a substantial amount of money for charity at the same time.

The 'Heal The World Foundation' meant that he was able to ensure that the money he raised ended up exactly where it was needed. The list of charities that were to benefit from the tour was impressive. Michael's public commitment to help children with AIDS also played a crucial role in highlighting a problem that many were only too willing to turn their backs on.

From the outset, the 'Dangerous' tour was to be the biggest and most spectacular rock tour ever seen.

Michael wanted to cover every continent on earth and play to audiences who had never had the chance to see him, in places like the former communist countries of Eastern Europe.

Rehearsals began early in 1992. One of the musicians picked for the tour says Michael was very strict about what his staff could and could not do while they were on the road.

"Everyone picked for the tour was told there'd be no drugs or alcohol and it was made clear that if they found that a problem, they should leave immediately. People have this image about rock 'n' roll tours but when you're on the road

with the biggest star on the planet, you don't go and do drugs or throw TVs out of hotel rooms because you are, in effect, representing Michael Jackson."

The first concerts were to be in Europe, and as dates were announced in England, France and Germany, it became clear that this was set to become another record breaking tour. Concerts at Europe's biggest venues sold out within hours. 200 thousand tickets for London's Wembley stadium were snapped up in two days.

Sales of 'Dangerous' were rocketing. Michael had also taken the unusual step of releasing up to half a dozen re-mixes of each single. The re-mix of 'Black or White' by C and C Music Factory was actually released as a separate single and sent the song back into the top twenty.

1992 also saw the release of the world's first rock documentary album about Michael Jackson. 'The Michael Jackson Story' was not an official album release by Michael

but was made by an independent production company who had set out two years earlier to establish the truth about his fascinating life.

They went to Gary, Indiana, and managed to interview the people who had known him in the very early days; friends, family and school teachers. They also spoke to staff at Motown who had looked after him through the '60s and '70s and managed to get rare interviews with some of those involved in the 'Dangerous' album.

This wealth of fascinating material was turned into a documentary lasting over an hour and was then released on cassette and a limited edition picture disc album. 'The Michael Jackson Story' was narrated by one of Britain's top radio presenters, Bob Lawrence.

"The response from fans who bought the album was amazing," says Bob. "When we started making it we just wanted to find out the real story about Michael, rather than all the rubbish printed in the press. I think it's fair to say that this album portrays him as a caring, loving and amazingly talented individual. The fans who bought it all told me how refreshing it was to hear the truth about Michael, and to hear it first hand from the people who know him best."

'The Michael Jackson Story' has many highlights; a trip to the school where Michael and his brothers won their first talent contest, a visit to the Motown studios where it all began and a journey to Michael's home town of Los Olivos to hear about the wonders of Neverland Valley.

Before the 'Dangerous' tour got underway, Michael took a well publicised holiday. With his forty strong entourage in tow, he set off for Africa. He visited several African countries and in each one was treated like royalty.

Gabon's President received Michael in a private audience, an honour usually reserved only for heads of state. He flew his private jet to Woleu-Ntem where crowds of young fans and traditional dancers

Michael visited comedian Benny Hill in hospital just two months before he died.
"You're my hero," he told Benny.

The results of one of Michael's spending sprees at Hamleys toystore in London.

gave him a spectacular welcome. He was then crowned King of the Agni tribe. Michael seemed to be having a wonderful time, yet, like all his activities, the African trip also had its bizarre side. Everywhere Michael went, he seemed to be holding his nose. The first rumour was that he could not stand the smell. The second was that the heat was melting his nose. While the fuss continued, Michael suddenly announced that he was cutting the trip short because of urgent business at home.

Within hours he was gone, curiously not heading for California, but England.

Michael flew into London and moved into the plush Dorchester hotel for five days. It soon became clear that if he had left Africa for business, it was only the business of creating more publicity.

Michael's stay in London was one massive media circus. He arrived with his ten year old cousin, Brett, and spent his time on a series of trips to record and toy shops, the Madame Tussaud's waxworks and comedian Benny Hill, who was in hospital after a heart attack. Benny was one of Michael's favourite comedians and he was heartbroken when he died two months later.

The highlight of his short stay was undoubtedly the hour he spent shopping in the massive Hamleys toystore. Michael had the store closed while he and Brett were shown around. They left with a fortune in toys and games, paid for by Michael's bodyguard with the ever present credit card.

Although his stay in London was supposed to be 'private', Michael's every step was followed by an army of press photographers. He happily obliged by continuing to hold his nose and cowering in the hotel doorway when the fans' hysteria got too much.

The loyal fans camped outside The Dorchester hotel day and night. Their patience was rewarded when Michael and Brett made an appearance on the balcony, waving and throwing paper darts at the crowd below. On his last night Michael even wrote the fans a letter:

"I truly, truly love you all very much. I love England. You will always be in my heart for ever and ever.

I am going to sleep now because I have an early flight back to America.

I adore you all. I love you. Michael Jackson."

Beneath his signature he wrote: "Let's heal the world together. The children, the animals and ecology. M.J."

And in the bottom corner of the hotel notepaper he added: "I want to hear that you have my letter. Goodnight."

The fans sang Michael a couple of choruses of 'Heal The World' to prove that they did indeed have the letter. Then they let him go to sleep.

Apart from the many stories it produced, the trip to London is interesting because it highlights Michael's immense talent in generating endless publicity at exactly the right time. If he had really wanted a private visit to Britain, there were far more secluded places for him to stay than a hotel in the heart of London. The simple fact was that the first European dates for the 'Dangerous' tour were about to be announced and Michael wanted to ensure that he was front page news when tickets went on sale. He was, and the concerts were an immediate sell out.

Those who saw the early rehearsals for the 'Dangerous' tour in the Spring of 1992 soon realised that Michael had once again surpassed himself with a breathtaking stage show that was to set new standards for rock tours.

On the road he worked as hard as ever. One of the musicians on the tour says he was amazed at Michael's energy.

"I've never seen anyone work so hard. During rehearsals he spent all morning with the dancers, then he'd come and practise with the band right up until 10 o'clock at night. It was the same every day and I never saw him ill. I walked into his room one day and he'd been dancing for eight hours, practising new steps in front of the mirror."

Even on his days off, another musician says that Michael never seemed to rest.

"On the days we weren't playing he was still busy, negotiating deals or checking video footage of the concerts. He's always on top of everything. That's part of the reason for his success."

All of those who work with Michael agree that he is a strange combination of characters. Quiet and shy in public, a complete extrovert on stage and a shrewd decision maker when it comes to business.

"He's a lot different in person to how he is on stage," says one of his musicians. "Sometimes he's just a complete clown. He has food fights. He loves joking around and just having a laugh. He loves his family. When Janet Jackson or his cousins come to see him he's just a relaxed, family loving guy, but when it comes to business, that disappears and it's 100 per cent concentration."

The same quiet determination that Michael uses to control his business affairs extends to his

Michael and his cousin, Brett, make an appearance for the fans on their hotel balcony while (below) lookalikes hold their own Michael Jackson concert outside the hotel entrance.

relationship with his musicians. He is very easy-going but always expects the best.

"The pressure you feel from Michael to be perfect every night is intense," says one of the band members. "It's good though because all of a sudden your perfection level rockets and you have more ability than you ever dreamt you had."

The organisation involved in a tour as massive as 'Dangerous' is enormous. Truck loads of lighting, sound equipment and stage gear arrive at the venue several days ahead of Michael. The crew then work day and night to get everything ready in time.

Dozens of technicians, engineers, carpenters and lighting supervisors are needed to ensure that each show meets Michael's high standards.

Choreographers and dancers spend hours rehearsing to perfect their routines. The musicians spend the day of each concert rehearsing and setting up their equipment. Early in the afternoon, Michael will arrive casually dressed for the sound check. Wherever he goes he is surrounded by bodyguards. Many of them blend in with the crowds, their eyes constantly watching for possible trouble. Immediately surrounding Michael are his personal guards, headed by Bill Bray who has been with him since he was a child. Michael has perfected the art of surviving the crowd hysteria that seems to follow him wherever he goes. It basically consists of crouching down, shielding his face with his hands and relying on the bodyguards to get him through.

Also on the tour is Michael's entourage of cooks, hairdressers, make-up artists, wardrobe assistants and personal staff. A team of press officers ensure that the stories that get to the media are carefully selected and timed to ensure maximum impact.

Michael makes no secret of the fact that he often finds the gruelling schedule and pressure of touring a strain. The moments on stage are wonderful, but the travelling and constant attention focused on him can be an enormous burden. Nevertheless, Michael would not have it any other way. He tells friends that he was put on earth to entertain and that his concerts are his direct link to the world.

"I'm totally at home on the stage. That's where I live. That's where I was born. That's where I'm safe."

As Michael Jackson's amazing success reaches new heights, the world tries harder and harder to unravel the mystery of his strange lifestyle. The harder we try, the further we will get from the truth. Michael will continue to encourage the mystique because the interest it creates is fundamental to his success. At the same time, one of the aims of the 'Dangerous' tour was to turn attention away from his personality and focus it on his music, to prove that Michael Jackson's performances are light years ahead of anyone else. Those who have seen the shows are left in little doubt.

As for Michael's apparent weirdness, that is best summed up by one of his closest friends, musician Greg Phillinganes.

"There are many different sides to him just as there are many different sides to all of us. He's just another guy trying to express himself and fit in the world. He can be very nice, there are obviously things that make him angry but he's basically a good man with a good soul. The other thing about Michael is that he's a very strong person. For all the junk that he's been through, for all the hype, he's been strong enough to survive without the aid of drink and drugs. Most people can't do that and that's the thing I admire him most for. He's been through a lot of bad times but he's never taken drugs. As for his eccentricities, I'm not defending them or criticising them, but there are a lot of people who do far whackier things than Mickey will ever dream about."

For Michael, his never ending quest for musical perfection will continue. His determination to use every ounce of energy he has to help the world's children will stay with him for the rest of his life. What form this takes, only time will tell. There will be more albums and Michael is keen to get involved further in the world of films, both producing movies and acting in them. Above all, he will never stop performing. Whatever the strains of touring, Michael Jackson's concerts are the moments when his real personality shines through; pure talent, pure energy and pure love:

"When I stand on that stage and look out, I see every race and they're all waving and holding hands, smiling and dancing. That to me is accomplishing everything. That's the biggest reward for me, more than money, just bringing all those people together. You see kids out there dancing, as well as the grown ups and the grandparents. All ages, all colours. That's what's great. That's what keeps me going."

MICHAEL JACKSON FACTFILE

1958
29 AUGUST. MICHAEL JACKSON IS BORN IN GARY, INDIANA.

1963
FIVE YEAR OLD MICHAEL PERFORMS 'CLIMB EV'RY MOUNTAIN' FROM 'THE SOUND OF MUSIC' IN FRONT OF HIS CLASS AT SCHOOL...IT IS HIS FIRST PUBLIC PERFORMANCE.

1964
MICHAEL STARTS REHEARSING WITH HIS BROTHERS.

1965
THE JACKSON 5 WIN THEIR FIRST TALENT CONTEST AT ROOSEVELT HIGH SCHOOL IN GARY.

1966
THE GROUP MAKE THEIR DEBUT AT MR LUCKY'S NIGHTCLUB IN GARY AND PERFORM AT CLUBS AND COLLEGES IN CHICAGO AND INDIANA.

1968
STEELTOWN RECORDS IN GARY RELEASE TWO JACKSON 5 SINGLES; 'BIG BOY' AND 'WE DON'T HAVE TO BE OVER 21'.

THE GROUP AUDITION AT THE MOTOWN STUDIOS IN DETROIT.

1969
THE JACKSON 5 ARE SIGNED TO MOTOWN. MICHAEL AND HIS BROTHERS MOVE TO CALIFORNIA.

1970
'I WANT YOU BACK' IS THE GROUP'S FIRST NUMBER ONE.

1971-72
THE JACKSON 5 TOUR THE WORLD.
MICHAEL'S FIRST SOLO NUMBER ONE - 'BEN'.

1975
THE JACKSON 5 LEAVE MOTOWN AND SIGN TO CBS/EPIC RECORDS. BECAUSE OF A LEGAL ROW THEY CHANGE THEIR NAME TO 'THE JACKSONS'.

1977
THE GROUP FLY TO ENGLAND TO JOIN THE CELEBRATIONS FOR QUEEN ELIZABETH'S SILVER JUBILEE.

1978
MICHAEL STARS WITH DIANA ROSS IN THE FILM, 'THE WIZ'.

1979
'OFF THE WALL' ALBUM IS RELEASED. IT GOES ON TO SELL SIX MILLION COPIES.

1980
MICHAEL WINS HIS FIRST GRAMMY FOR 'DON'T STOP 'TIL YOU GET ENOUGH'.

1981
MICHAEL RECORDS 'THE GIRL IS MINE' WITH PAUL McCARTNEY.

1982
'THRILLER' IS RELEASED.

1983
MICHAEL'S HISTORIC PERFORMANCE OF 'BILLIE JEAN' AT THE MOTOWN 25TH ANNIVERSARY SHOW.

'BILLIE JEAN' AND 'BEAT IT' HIT THE NUMBER ONE SPOT.

THE 'THRILLER' VIDEO IS SHOWN FOR THE FIRST TIME ON MTV.

1984
MICHAEL'S HAIR CATCHES FIRE DURING FILMING FOR A PEPSI COMMERCIAL.

'THRILLER' IS ENTERED INTO THE GUINNESS BOOK OF RECORDS AS THE BEST SELLING ALBUM OF ALL TIME.

MICHAEL WINS EIGHT GRAMMY AWARDS.

THE JACKSONS' VICTORY TOUR ENDS WITH THE BROTHERS' LAST SHOW TOGETHER IN LOS ANGELES.

MICHAEL IS WELCOMED TO THE WHITE HOUSE BY PRESIDENT REAGAN.

1985
MICHAEL WRITES U.S.A. FOR AFRICA'S 'WE ARE THE WORLD' WITH LIONEL RICHIE.

SCENES OF HYSTERIA AT MADAME TUSSAUD'S IN LONDON WHEN HE ARRIVES TO UNVEIL HIS WAXWORK.

MICHAEL PAYS 47.5 MILLION DOLLARS FOR THE PUBLISHING RIGHTS TO THE BEATLES' SONGS.

1986
15 MILLION DOLLAR SPONSORSHIP DEAL SIGNED WITH PEPSI.

REPORTS THAT MICHAEL IS SLEEPING IN AN OXYGEN CHAMBER TO HELP HIM LIVE TO 150.

1987
RELEASE OF THE 'BAD' ALBUM.

MICHAEL LEAVES THE JEHOVAH'S WITNESSES.

REPORTS THAT HE WANTS TO BUY THE REMAINS OF THE ELEPHANT MAN.

THE 'BAD' TOUR GETS UNDERWAY.

1988
THE TOUR BREAKS RECORDS WORLDWIDE. AT ONE OF HIS CONCERTS IN LONDON, MICHAEL MEETS PRINCE CHARLES AND PRINCESS DIANA.

THE 'MOONWALKER' FILM IS RELEASED TOGETHER WITH MICHAEL'S AUTOBIOGRAPHY 'MOONWALK'.

1989
MANAGER FRANK DILEO IS SACKED.

MICHAEL MOVES TO HIS NEW HOME, NEVERLAND VALLEY.

1990
MICHAEL IS NAMED ENTERTAINER OF THE DECADE. HE IS ONE OF THE MOURNERS AT THE FUNERAL OF TEENAGE AIDS VICTIM, RYAN WHITE.

MICHAEL IS RUSHED TO HOSPITAL AFTER A HEART ATTACK SCARE. IT TURNS OUT TO BE CAUSED BY STRESS.

1991
NEW MULTI MILLION DOLLAR RECORD CONTRACT SIGNED WITH SONY.

MADONNA IS MICHAEL'S ESCORT AT THE OSCARS.

'BLACK OR WHITE', MICHAEL'S FIRST SINGLE FOR THREE YEARS TOPS THE CHARTS WORLDWIDE.

HE APPEARS IN AN EPISODE OF 'THE SIMPSONS'.

'DANGEROUS' IS RELEASED.

1992-93
THE 'DANGEROUS' WORLD TOUR.

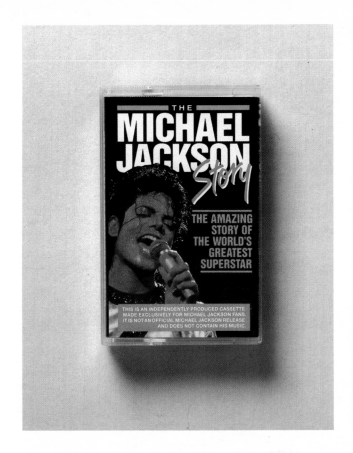

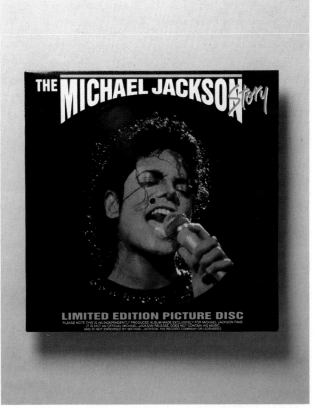

THE MICHAEL JACKSON STORY

AVAILABLE ON ALBUM AND CASSETTE

'The Michael Jackson Story' is an amazing one hour rock documentary telling the entire story of Michael's extraordinary life.

From material recorded in Indiana, Detroit, California and London, this album provides a unique insight into his career from the people who know him best. Now you can hear the real truth about Michael Jackson, including:

His early days as a childhood star.
The triumph of the 'Thriller' and 'Bad' years.
The making of 'Dangerous.'
Life on tour with the world's greatest live performer.

'The Michael Jackson Story' is available
on cassette and on a stunning, limited edition picture disc.
If your record shop does not have it in stock, they can order it for you.
Just give them the cassette or album catalogue number.

The Michael Jackson Story. Cassette, Catalogue number POWA MC1
The Michael Jackson Story. Picture Disc Album, Catalogue number POWA LP1
Distributed by Total.

MICHAEL JACKSON DISCOGRAPHY

SINGLES

	DATE OF RELEASE	USA	UK
BIG BOY*	1968	●	○
WE DON'T HAVE TO BE OVER 21*	1968	●	○
I WANT YOU BACK*	OCT 69	1	2
ABC*	FEB 70	1	8
THE LOVE YOU SAVE*	MAY 70	1	7
I'LL BE THERE*	AUG 70	1	4
MAMA'S PEARL*	JAN 71	2	25
NEVER CAN SAY GOODBYE*	MAR 71	2	33
MAYBE TOMORROW*	JUN 71	20	○
GOT TO BE THERE	OCT 71	4	5
SUGAR DADDY*	NOV 71	10	●
ROCKIN' ROBIN	FEB 72	2	3
LITTLE BITTY PRETTY ONE*	APR 72	13	●
I WANNA BE WHERE YOU ARE	MAY 72	16	○
LOOKIN' THROUGH THE WINDOWS*	JUN 72	16	9
AINT NO SUNSHINE	JUL 72	○	8
BEN	JUL 72	1	7
CORNER OF THE SKY*	OCT 72	18	○
DOCTOR MY EYES*	FEB 73	○	9
HALLELUJAH DAY*	FEB 73	28	20
WITH A CHILD'S HEART	APR 73	50	○
GET IT TOGETHER*	AUG 73	28	○
SKYWRITER*	SEPT 73	○	25
DANCING MACHINE*	FEB 74	2	●
WHATEVER YOU GOT I WANT*	OCT 74	38	●
I AM LOVE*	DEC 74	15	●
WE'RE ALMOST THERE	FEB 75	54	○
JUST A LITTLE BIT OF YOU	APR 75	23	○
FOREVER CAME TODAY*	JUN 75	60	●
ENJOY YOURSELF**	NOV 76	6	42
SHOW YOU THE WAY TO GO**	APR 77	28	1
DREAMER**	JUL 77	○	22
GOIN' PLACES**	OCT 77	52	26
EVEN THOUGH YOU'RE GONE**	JAN 78	○	31
EASE ON DOWN THE ROAD (DUET WITH DIANA ROSS)	OCT 78	41	45
BLAME IT ON THE BOOGIE**	NOV 78	54	8
DESTINY**	DEC 78	○	39
SHAKE YOUR BODY (DOWN TO THE GROUND)**	JAN 79	7	4
YOU CAN'T WIN	JAN 79	81	○
DON'T STOP 'TIL YOU GET ENOUGH	JUL 79	1	3
ROCK WITH YOU	NOV 79	1	7
OFF THE WALL	FEB 80	10	7
SHE'S OUT OF MY LIFE	APR 80	10	3
GIRLFRIEND	JUL 80	○	41
LOVELY ONE**	SEPT 80	12	29
HEARTBREAK HOTEL**	DEC 80	22	44
ONE DAY IN YOUR LIFE	MAR 81	55	1
CAN YOU FEEL IT**	APR 81	77	6
WALK RIGHT NOW**	JUN 81	73	7
THE GIRL IS MINE (WITH PAUL McCARTNEY)	OCT 82	2	8
BILLIE JEAN	JAN 83	1	1
BEAT IT	MAR 83	1	3

	DATE OF RELEASE	USA	UK
WANNA BE STARTIN' SOMETHING	MAY 83	5	8
HUMAN NATURE	JUL 83	○	7
P.Y.T. (PRETTY YOUNG THING)	OCT 83	10	11
SAY, SAY, SAY (WITH PAUL McCARTNEY)	OCT 83	1	2
THRILLER	FEB 84	4	10
FAREWELL MY SUMMER LOVE	MAY 84	38	7
STATE OF SHOCK**	JUN 84	3	14
TORTURE**	AUG 84	17	26
BODY**	OCT 84	47	○
I JUST CAN'T STOP LOVING YOU	JUL 87	1	1
BAD	SEPT 87	1	3
THE WAY YOU MAKE ME FEEL	NOV 87	1	3
MAN IN THE MIRROR	FEB 88	1	21
I WANT YOU BACK 88- REMIX	MAR 88	○	8
DIRTY DIANA	JUL 88	1	4
ANOTHER PART OF ME	SEPT 88	11	15
SMOOTH CRIMINAL	NOV 88	7	8
LEAVE ME ALONE	FEB 89	○	2
LIBERIAN GIRL	JUL 89	○	13
BLACK OR WHITE	NOV 91	1	1
REMEMBER THE TIME	MAR 92	3	4

ALBUMS

This does not include the many compilations which are re-issues of old songs.

	DATE OF RELEASE	USA	UK
DIANA ROSS PRESENTS THE JACKSON 5*	DEC 69	5	16
ABC*	MAY 70	4	22
THIRD ALBUM*	SEPT 70	4	○
THE JACKSON 5 CHRISTMAS ALBUM*	OCT 70	1	○
MAYBE TOMORROW*	APR 71	1	●
GOIN' BACK TO INDIANA*	SEPT 71	16	●
JACKSON 5 GREATEST HITS*	DEC 71	12	26
GOT TO BE THERE	JAN 72	14	37
LOOKIN' THROUGH THE WINDOWS*	MAY 72	7	16
BEN	AUG 72	5	17
SKYWRITER*	MAR 73	44	○
MUSIC AND ME	APR 73	92	○
GET IT TOGETHER*	SEPT 73	100	○
DANCING MACHINE*	SEPT 74	16	○
FOREVER MICHAEL	JAN 75	101	○
MOVING VIOLATION*	MAY 75	36	○
THE JACKSONS**	NOV 76	36	54
GOIN' PLACES**	OCT 77	63	45
DESTINY**	DEC 78	11	33
OFF THE WALL	AUG 79	3	5
TRIUMPH**	OCT 80	10	13
JACKSONS LIVE**	NOV 81	30	53
THRILLER	DEC 82	1	1
VICTORY**	JUL 84	4	3
BAD	SEPT 87	1	1
DANGEROUS	NOV 91	1	1

KEY:
* WITH THE JACKSON 5
** WITH THE JACKSONS
○ NOT RELEASED
● DID NOT CHART